Who Am I Now?

Realign Your Home and Life

by Kate Varness, CPO-CD®, COC®, MA

Although the author has made every effort to ensure that the information in this book was correct at press time, the author does not assume and hereby disclaims any liability to any party for any loss, damage, or disruption caused by errors or omissions, whether such errors or omissions result from negligence, accident, or any other cause.

This book is not intended as a substitute for the medical advice of physicians. The reader should regularly consult a physician in matters relating to his/her health and particularly with respect to any symptoms that may require diagnosis or medical attention.

This book is dedicated to my clients and audience members,

who have taught me about bravery and real change,

and given me the opportunity to have a meaningful vocation.

TABLE OF CONTENTS

INTRODUCTION

"If something is going to happen to me, I want to be there."
Albert Camus

Who Am I?

How would you finish the sentence, "I am...?" You could fill in the surface details of your life (name, age, gender, physical characteristics, address) or explain your deepest philosophical aspects (what are your values and life purpose). Or, you could answer the question by looking at the progression of your life from childhood until now in connection to life transitions (changing careers, caring for a parent, kids are in college, retiring, downsizing, etc.). We will begin with life transitions because your life is shifting or needing to shift, and you want clarity, ease, and alignment.

So, what are life transitions and how do they relate to the "I am" question? Life transitions are life-changing events that cause us to re-examine who we are and how we function with the shifting demands of the new situation. Some life transitions are expected, others are unexpected. Some are self-driven, while others are imposed from outside. Many of us experience life transitions in the first half of our lives that require us to consciously articulate how we are shifting: "I am going to college," "I am getting married," "I am preparing for my baby." These changes tend to be aspirational, meaning we have chosen them.

In the second half of our lives, we encounter life transitions that may or may not be ones we aspire to. Whether or not we act with courage may change as we age. Life transitions early in life included excitement and perhaps some fear. However, the fear was overcome with the courage (idiocy?) of youth. Life transitions later in life still involve excitement, but the fear factor combines with hesitancy (wisdom?) gained from years in the school of hard knocks, a.k.a. life. Life has taught us that decisions have consequences that can overshadow the excitement of doing something new. Hesitancy is both a good thing, in that it keeps us from doing the stupid stuff young people do, and a bad thing, because it keeps us stuck in what is familiar rather than leap into the unknown.

Since "stuck" is probably a feeling that led you to pick up this book, let's look at an example of someone in a life transition. Lainey has been a nurse for thirty years. Her kids have flown the nest, and she is divorced. While nursing has been a wonderful career, she no longer feels the spark to work at the clinic. She wonders if maybe there's another chapter of her life and career that would excite her. She's ten, maybe fifteen, years from retirement. What would a new direction look like? Does she really want to search for a new job? Going back to school sounds awful to her, but so does fifteen more years at the same job. Can she risk change financially? What will others think?

Lainey stands in a liminal place. Liminal is just a fancy word to describe an in-between place. She's on the threshold of making a change...perhaps. In reality, she could stay on the doorstep of change for a very long time. There are three options: she can stay fixed at the in-between place, paralyzed by indecision; she can be pushed into change by something that may or may not send her in a positive direction; or she can step onto a path leading away from her current state, even if she doesn't know all the details. I call this last option a "leap of faith." Needless to say, Lainey is a bundle of mixed emotions. Can you relate?

The Hero's Journey

You are here because you have those mixed feelings and want relief. On the one hand, you are sick and tired of being stuck. You know something is off-track. Your life is sending you signals to wake up to the new reality. Perhaps your home is too cluttered, you can't keep up the cleaning or mowing the lawn of your big house, or you look down at your morning pills and think, "How the hell did I get so many medications?"

On the other hand, you're experiencing inklings of possibility. Perhaps you are no longer responsible for caring for other people or are free from the daily grind of working. A little voice inside whispers a desire to go on adventures, to move, or to redefine how you are living.

These mixed emotions are totally normal, though maybe that's not reassuring. Feeling so unsettled may make you think you are doing something wrong. What if I told you it means you are doing something right? Are you familiar with the concept of the "hero's journey?" Certainly, you have seen plenty of movies or read books that contain it. The *Harry Potter* series, *Lord of the Rings*, and *Star Wars* are just a few examples of how a character sets out on a quest, encounters difficulties, learns about him or herself, wants to quit but sticks with it, and emerges victorious—although transformed—at the end.

Your life is a hero's journey. I'm assuming you want to be the hero of your story and not just a passive bystander to circumstances, right? It's up to you to decide. Can you be the hero of your story? It will require you to wake up and to step bravely into the unknown. Truth be told, it isn't totally unknown. No one arrives at this point in life without encountering some major challenges. The fact that you are reading this indicates that you've weathered storms in your life. You don't weather storms without becoming somewhat resilient and resourceful.

What does it mean to be resilient and resourceful? It means growing up with neglectful parents, but learning skills to have good relationships. It means getting laid off, but figuring out how to provide for your family. It means having a sick child who you nursed back to health. The challenges and triumphs of your life may not have ever been cataloged by you. Make a list of times you were faced with a challenge and discovered a way through it. Even small things count. Let's say you scored poorly on the ACT, then found test training, practiced for hours, and improved your score. What personal qualities were needed to improve your test score?

Consider a situation where your phone falls into a lake, causing you to lose information about your contacts, which have not been backed up. You don't just give up ever having a phone again. Instead, you investigate ways to gather the information again. This takes resourcefulness and resilience, something you already possess and will use during this realignment process.

My intention is to encourage you. The word "encourage" stems from the Latin word "cor," meaning heart. Living life with heart involves fulfilling your purpose, no matter how messy it might be. We all know that courage means to be brave. Our work here won't give you courage because you already have courage within you. I aim to remind you of what you already possess. We will be in courage together. I will provide opportunities and tools to help your bravery emerge; however, none of this is possible unless you do the work.

That starts with you committing to be the hero of your life. Will you answer the call?

My Leap of Faith

Let me tell you about a time I showed courage. I'll begin with Prince's song, "Party Like It's 1999" playing in the background. My husband, a tech guy, was on call to respond to potential Y2K issues. For you young'uns, Y2K refers to the concern that computer systems would get messed up when the first two digits of the year code changed from nineteen to twenty. As I headed into my final semester to complete my Master's degree in English Literature, I contemplated my future. Would I go on to get my Ph.D. and teach college? I always imagined myself as "the cool professor" wearing a tweed jacket, with an entourage of adoring students, hosting monthly parties at my house. Nearing the end of my Master's program, this expected future suddenly wasn't.

As a teaching assistant, I discovered that only about two students out of thirty were really interested in the required writing courses I taught. While some had mediocre interest, at least a third of students slumped in the back row with pulled-down baseball hats covering their closed eyes. How much of an impact was I really making?

I was in the midst of writing my Master's thesis—a rollicking examination of how three leading Victorian thinkers responded to an upstart art and literary group called the Pre-Raphaelites. Sounds fascinating, I know. If I pursued a Ph.D., publication in literary journals would be critical. At some point, I had the realization that very few people worldwide cared about this topic. Was this what I wanted for my career?

The last point of internal conflict came after witnessing the hiring process for literature professors. Well-qualified candidates—all post-PhD, some having written books and many having prestigious fellowships—had difficulty finding a tenure-track position due to a scarcity of openings. In addition to the pressure of a competitive job field, applicants experienced pressure from their potential department. This happened when applicants presented sample lectures to faculty and experienced a version of hazing by department denizens seeking to demonstrate their own superiority. Maybe every job has this dynamic. At the time it seemed more unwelcoming than collegial. In spite of doing well within my program, something inside said, "Push the pause button."

At this point, my husband and I had been married five years and we thought it was a good time to have children. I was excited by the possibility of being their primary caregiver and was able to do that financially due to my husband's job. Our baby girl arrived in 2000, then a baby boy two years later. Being an at-home mother proved harder than I ever imagined, but my heart affirmed the value of that choice. In the midst of the steep parenthood learning curve, I noticed internal stirrings about career and where I might be headed in addition to mothering. At that moment, though, I was content with knowing that the pause button was pushed.

Fast forward to 2004. We considered having baby number three, but our house was too small. This was one of those liminal places I mentioned before. Four years had passed since I finished my Master's. Would I pursue a Ph.D.? I suspected that professorship was not for me, but what would the replacement be? I really didn't know, and that was unsettling, so I decided to go with what I did know: having a third child and wanting to move.

I began the process of evaluating our things and packing them up. When I came to my two-drawer file cabinet filled with research articles gathered during my Master's degree, the fork in the road became clear. I could either move the entire cabinet, thus delaying a decision about the papers and the possibility of being a college professor, or I could face the decision. If you don't already know, stuff isn't just stuff; it represents history, hopes, and dreams— real or unmet. These files were my possible ticket to my tweed jacket and adoring students. To toss the papers meant acknowledging that the path was closed. What was I going to do? While I didn't know what would replace my vision, I had a very strong hunch that my old vision wasn't going to happen.

sometimes Stuff isn't just stuff

In those moments standing in front of the file cabinet, I decided that it was okay to not know. Believe me, that felt scary. It also felt brave. I decided that the research I collected could be researched again if I changed my mind. In fact, I would need fresh research if I decided to pursue professorship. I kept only the best of the best of my paper files that could not be saved another way. I liberated myself of forty inches of files, keeping only two inches. I believed that I would be okay. And I was.

Actually, I was more than okay. Within the next three weeks, we got pregnant, sold our existing house, and bought a new one. It was during this time that I became aware of my current profession of home organizing. For four years, I had been watching shows on HGTV featuring professional organizers, yet I had never considered it as a potential career. Why not? The answer: I had been holding too tightly onto the old vision of me in my tweed

Too stuffed, there is no room to see possibility to see something different.

jacket with adoring students. There was no room for me to see the possibility of something different. Before, I was afraid to take the leap of faith, then, when I stepped into the unknown and discovered things I hadn't even considered, I realized the results were better than anything I could have dreamed up on my own.

This is how I learned the life principle that if your life is too stuffed, you have no room for new blessings. In other words, if you want something new, you must first let go of what is extra, what is not serving you. Although I cannot guarantee that you will win the lottery by cleaning out your shoe collection, I can affirm that letting go of old dreams gives you space to notice what is possible, as well as helps you pay attention to your current experience. Contrast the closed fist with the open hand; which can grasp better that thing that is headed in your direction?

Until I became open, I couldn't see what had been right in front of me all along. Suddenly, there I was, entertaining the idea that I would enjoy helping people get their homes organized. After an internet search to see what professional home organizing entailed, I found that that the National Association of Productivity and Organizing Professionals℠ (www.NAPO.net) had a chapter near me. The first weekend workshop I attended deepened my interest. Their annual conference was within driving distance too, so I signed up, spending money on a career without having earned a dollar.

My internal compass indicated that I should follow the path as it unfolded. One step at a time, the direction continued to be confirmed. Take note: what allowed any of this to happen was me letting go of the old dream without fully specifying a new dream. What guided me was being attuned to what I knew about myself at that moment, then continuing to check in with how the exploration process resonated with me and carried me forward.

Life is not static. I'm nearing another transition. Actually, there are multiple transitions. Those babies are headed to college. My parents are ailing. It's time to think about being nimble and to evaluate where I find my spark. So we're on this journey together. Let's look at the signs that it's time to take stock and what to consider as you move into a new stage.

You are Here, But Are You Here?

feel free

Your home has begun to feel a bit claustrophobic. Too much stuff. Too many obligations. You want to feel free like some of your friends who have moved from the homes they raised their kids in. You don't want to end up like your friend who died from a heart attack and whose kids rolled up a dumpster and trashed the home's contents. You want to travel, to get your photos in order, to volunteer at the food pantry. These are things you haven't gotten to. Why not? You retired a year ago. You have the time, except you still feel quite busy. Every time you have tried to sort through your things you get overwhelmed and don't know where to start. You start a donation box, then worry about wanting the items you put into it.

The whole process feels hard and disorienting. You realize that things have changed in your life. The kids are adults. You no longer have a nine-to-five job. In a way, you are standing at the map of your life knowing you are here, at this stage in life and that it is the same, but it is also different. The question is, are you here? Has your mind fully shifted to who you are now?

process feels hard disorienting

In times of transition, you must pause and locate yourself. The pause allows you to locate where you are. The biggest mistake people make in times of transition is to just plow ahead using old information that applied to a previous transition. Once you define the new information about your circumstances, you must accept it to be true. Assessing it can be easier than accepting it, though. Accepting that something has happened does not mean you have to like it. Acceptance acknowledges that it is—it exists. You can be present to the joy in your life right now and gain future joy by walking through the gateway of accepting your life's reality. Resisting continues a mismatch between your life, your home, and your habits. Resisting extends feeling frustrated and disoriented.

The Truth(s) Will Set You Free

Your path to self-rediscovery is laid out in this book in three sections filled with stories, exercises, strategies, and concepts to ponder. The first section, Realign Habits, examines habits that may be no longer helpful, the signs of being misaligned, and ways to get unstuck. Section two, Realign Vocation, looks at a career change, with its ripple effect on your home, relationships, and self-concept. Finally, in section three, Realign Roles, we look at some of the changes that come at us externally—ones we haven't chosen, but which alter everything—and the skills needed to navigate through these storms. Each section is designed to deepen your self-awareness, encouraging you to participate as the hero of your life who can assess what is happening now, what parts of yourself you will carry forward, and what needs to open to new possibilities.

I'm not one for platitudes—those pat phrases people utter to others and to themselves when something bad happens—because platitudes dishonor the messy complexity of the human experience. I realize that some find comfort in

messy complexity of Human experience

Facing the truth leads to self-efficacy

these kinds of statements. If that describes you, then maybe the processes of this book are not right for you. I believe the truth, however complicated, leads to powerful self-efficacy and life happiness when paired with the skills needed to see the truth and a supportive community to share the journey. Find a friend or two to join you on this journey, either in person, by phone, or by video conference. Ask your book club or your church friends or your coffee group to meet over a few weeks to complete it.

The stories in these pages center on the truth of how people operate in real life. These experiences are complex, the kind of moments you experience, but tell no one. Complex situations are not solved by simple solutions, nor are they fixed overnight. Not only do I dislike platitudes, but I also dislike unrealistic, impractical solutions. We are getting to the heart of things with our examples and our solutions. This book takes you through a process informed by what I call the "Five Truths," which are based on fifteen years plus of helping people professionally and four decades on this planet. I introduce these five truths below and will explain how they inform the realignment process in Chapter 2.

Truth #1: People can see the situation more clearly with others than with themselves. _. Fresh eyes, talk it out_

Over years of giving presentations, I've observed that people like to figure out other people's problems, and have a harder time identifying solutions for their own problems. Let's call this the "Dear Abby effect" in homage to the long-running advice column started by Pauline Phillips in 1956. Don't we all love to give advice? That's why each chapter will have a story developed based on years of seeing, listening, and reading. If you see yourself in these stories, it's because I have a secret camera placed in your house. Just kidding! If you can relate, it's because the story illustrates a common issue—meaning you have lots of company in your very normal struggle. You get to be the expert observer to each story to hone your observation skills and then gently turn them to your own situation. Each chapter will allow for information gathering on your current lifestyle.

Truth #2: People do not change until the pain of staying the same exceeds the pain of changing.

We'll look at the cost of the mismatch between continuing to live with old habits and skills when life points to developing new solutions. One important step in the Stages of Change model is to raise one's consciousness about the pain of staying the same. You will not change until the pain of staying the same exceeds the pain of changing. In other words, people can get used to some pretty dysfunctional situations for the sake of doing what they know, until, one day, they just have had enough. The scales get tipped towards being brave enough to try a different approach—in spite of the discomfort of doing things differently—because they can't take the known, but crappy, situation anymore. This truth aims to raise your awareness of the pain of the situation to encourage you to be courageous and try something different.

Truth #3: Unless people voice their worst fear, they will not make a change.

That's why each chapter has a section called "When Zombies Attack." In case you didn't know, a zombie apocalypse is when the undead rise to take over civilization, infecting humans with their zombie virus, thus creating more zombies. Society shuts down. Non-infected humans gather in safe zones and try to survive. Think *Night of the Living Dead* (1968). It sounds ridiculous, and it is. However, a decision-making process requires you to dig deeper and face your fears. Instead of stopping the process when you meet perceived resistance, you will explore further to see if the feared outcome will really happen. What if there are monsters under your bed? You should at least turn on a light to look. We can look together. What if the worst-case scenario of a zombie apocalypse comes true? Think of what you must to know to survive. In most cases, you already possess the interior fortitude to survive. The world is not going to end by letting an object go. But you must take a peek at that worst fear, or risk getting stuck in fear purgatory.

Truth #4: If you cannot imagine a better future, you will not step out of the past.

If someone thinks the best part of her life is over, then why in the world would she give up items that represent that time? You will not be able to look honestly at your present needs until you can entertain the possibility that there is a joy to be experienced right now and in the future. Western society tells us that people lose relevance as they age. That's baloney. Consider how Baby Boomers (people born 1945-1964) have changed the United States at every stage of their lives. More hospitals were built to accommodate a surge in population, then more schools and bigger houses. Now Baby Boomers are changing what it means to thrive in older adulthood. So what's the process to reassess and reinvent oneself for the final third of life? Each chapter will present an opportunity to create a new vision for that—one you can get excited about. As you solidify your vision, you will feel more confident in letting go of old ways of being. You can still honor and enjoy your past memories, but you won't be imprisoned in them.

Truth #5: You require three things to be successful: a clear goal; a specific time/date to do it; and an accountability partner.

Here's the good news: you don't have to figure it out on your own. This book is designed to take you through the process of figuring out who you are now, coming to a sense of peace about it, and then taking action to match your home to your present reality. You can complete the workbook on your own, but I encourage you to do it with a friend, a group of friends, or in a therapeutic setting. Having others participate can provide support as you tackle tough spots and celebrate victories. To successfully navigate change, you want to speak about what is working and tweak what is not, and that's pretty hard to do alone.

Most importantly, moving through the book with others will provide accountability. As you know all too well, purchasing exercise equipment is not the same as using it. The same is true with this book. You will not benefit unless you read it and create accountability to support your goals. Accountability gets you started and pulls you through to completion. It involves being specific about what you will do, when it will happen, and who, besides yourself, cares about completing each step. These components of accountability are a non-negotiable aspect of your success. Gaining good accountability habits is especially important if you have had trouble following through in the past. Each story's project and habit action plans will model how to create accountability. The final part of each chapter will focus on getting specific with your action and habit plan for different areas of the home.

I intend this book to be interactive. Many of you do not like to write directly in a book, so I've created a free, printable companion workbook with the exercises, discovery questions, and blank versions of the action and habit plans. Go to https://www.greenlightorganizing.com/workbook/ to download your companion workbook at no additional cost to you. Now, go forth on your self-rediscovery! Step bravely away from the clutter and the pain of what's not working into new possibilities.

Section 1: Realign Habits

CHAPTER 1

Habits, Alignment, Transitions, Oh My!

"Wherever you are is the entry point."
Kabir

Habits

The word I most closely associate with the word habit is bad, as in "bad habit." Perhaps this is true for you also. Countless articles and books are dedicated to changing habits—especially those habits deemed unhealthy. Cultural sayings around habits fall into two categories: those referring to "kicking" or "breaking" a bad habit, and those describing the grip of habits upon us. If someone is a "creature of habit," he or she is comforted by the predictable routine of habitual behavior. The idiom that most applies to our work in this book—"force of habit"—describes habits as those automatic behaviors that may cause us to impulsively follow routine rather than respond to what current circumstances require.

"Force of habit" behavior leads to misalignment of your *knowledge* (which includes skills and habits), your *life stage* (the life demands and physical realities of your age/stage), and *your stuff* (what's in your home and how it is set up).

Align for a Successful Transition

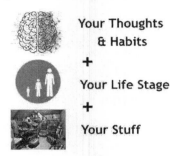

Your Thoughts
& Habits
+
Your Life Stage
+
Your Stuff

Alignment

The process of aligning a vehicle's wheels offers a wonderful metaphor for life realignment. In life and in cars, ignoring misalignment leads to unhappy consequences. Sure, you can ignore it for a while, white-knuckling the steering wheel to correct the car pulling to the left. Your extra effort at steering masks the fact that your wheels are wearing unevenly, dangerously, and unpredictably. But who has time to take a car in for service? Can you really trust the mechanic anyway? It all feels a bit overwhelming, so you put off servicing your car until an emergency forces you to address the problem. Many people try to ignore their life misalignment too, until it can be pushed aside no longer.

You may be able to fix the problem with simple adjustments—like evenly inflating the tires. In other cases, adjustments involve complex steps in multiple areas. When it comes to misalignment in life, you will also make simple or complex adjustments. Your initial assessment means taking stock of the basic facts of your life: your age, health, interests, activities, relationships, and other factors associated with functioning. Accurate assessment and—

more importantly—accepting the assessment, helps the process proceed faster.

Realignment isn't a one-size-fits-all process. Just as vehicle specifications vary, so do people. You have had many years to discover what works or doesn't for your optimal functioning. One alignment problem in people is an inability to decipher their true wishes about a situation or thing. Not recognizing your true wishes makes decisions feel paralyzing and letting go fear-filled. Perhaps you have been a people pleaser who never had a good sense of your personal preferences. Or, you may have known what you wanted at an earlier life stage, but pushed it aside to care for someone else. Tuning into and honoring your own intuition and desires allows you to reclaim being the best expert on you. Your self-determination isn't at the mercy of someone else; you control it. An expert writes the instruction manual on herself, which doesn't make her selfish; it empowers her to be the person she is meant to be. The exercises and stories in the coming chapters will help you reconnect to your true wishes.

A car alignment specialist knows that adjusting one part affects other parts. Let's look at just two alignment areas: toe and camber. When a mechanic tweaks the tire's toe position, he tests and reassesses each wheel individually and in relationship with the others. For life realignment, you will tweak one area, which will affect other areas. It's a gradual process of adjusting, then testing, trying something new, then seeing how it feels, all the time letting the results be what they are, without judgment, without perfectionism. Does your mechanic say, "I'm so angry that this car has an improper toe. Why do tires get off kilter anyway? It's not fair!" I think not. A

Isn't a one size fits all process

mechanic doesn't assume blame for the problem, he observes the problem, noticing what's working or not. You, too, can notice your life habits, stuck spots, and success points as a curious observer.

When a mechanic adjusts a vehicle's camber, each wheel is measured using a right triangle which is first aligned with the ground. In life realignment, other people's collective experience can be a reference point. I don't mean that you must adopt an individual person's experience: if Aunt Sally says the only way through grief is to pretend the loss didn't happen, that might not resonate with you (or frankly, anyone but Aunt Sally). I'm referring to the collective wisdom that inspires us to persevere in the midst of obstacles. It helps to be reminded of adjustments that have worked for others, and that you are not alone. This is especially true if you have experienced multiple personal traumas in quick succession. A car that has been in a major accident is more likely to have issues with the camber than one with normal wear and tear. Being in a car accident impacts the scope of the required adjustment and adds steps. Your unresolved trauma deserves attention. Trauma does not just disappear; it shows up in behavior whether you want it to or not, making it something that must be addressed.

When a car nears completion of the realignment process, it goes through a test drive, with the mechanic noticing how the alignment feels, and assessing whether further adjustments are warranted. In other words, it's a process of trial and error. Your small efforts will accumulate to get your home and life into optimal alignment, at least for who you are now. That the process feels effortful means you are on the right track, much like your arms may feel sore once you begin to lift weights. Habits that have been automatic (remember "force of habit?") are now consciously considered for change. That requires energy. Gathering your cohorts to participate helps you persevere during the alignment process. Teens call their friend group a "squad." Having a squad will encourage you to continue even when life feels a little messier, and you are trying new things.

Fluid and Crystallized Intelligence

The trial and error approach may seem more daunting as you age. Ever wonder why a two-year-old has less trouble using an electronic tablet than a seventy-five-year-old? The Cattell-Horn theory of fluid and crystallized intelligence explains this phenomenon. Fluid intelligence refers to problem-solving for a new challenge. Crystallized intelligence uses facts, prior learning, and experiences to solve problems. You build your crystallized intelligence until it peaks around age seventy; by contrast, fluid intelligence peaks in adolescence and begins to decline between the ages of thirty and forty.

In our example of the electronic tablet, a two-year-old is low on crystallized intelligence and must solve problems using fluid intelligence. She is not worried about breaking the iPad, whereas Grandpa, at age seventy-five, has had plenty of experiences where things went wrong. Grandpa would rather try to understand how to operate the iPad in reference to his experience using his desktop computer. He is not going to touch the screen willy-nilly just to see what will happen. Grandpa feels a bit panicked at having to navigate a novel situation that doesn't fit into his wealth of crystallized intelligence.

The concepts of fluid and crystallized intelligence help to understand and to navigate realignment successfully. If you have been plugging along, building your crystallized intelligence, and suddenly you notice that life has changed pretty significantly, you likely feel overwhelmed. How will you solve what looks like a whole new problem? The answer is to look at how you have been successful in the past. Tap into similar situations, analyze how you handled them, and duplicate that process, and you will feel much more confident. Another option is to enlist the help of young people who are peaking in their fluid intelligence. They naturally think outside the box, and they may illuminate a path that you couldn't have imagined. Also, they may benefit from your crystallized intelligence. Enlist them to help you feel brave—maybe you can touch the screen willy-nilly—and not stuck in limited thinking. It's worth a try, isn't it?

Life Transitions Bring a Mix of Emotions

We all experience life transitions. Life transitions elicit a mix of emotions: happy or sad, elated or disappointed, energized or confused, to name a few. Consider the life change of retirement.

For years, Leann sat behind her desk at work, dreaming of all the things she wouldn't do once she was retired. No more dragging her body out of bed too early. No more standstills on the freeway traveling to and from her job. No more dealing with her coworker Dennis, who critiqued anything he saw. No more dreading the possibility of her lunch getting stolen from the breakroom fridge. Leann would finally get to read all day, or garden, maybe travel, and she definitely would catch up on house projects she hadn't had time to do while working full-time.

Once Leann had been retired a year and a half, she discovered retirement was much different than she expected. Her body woke up early no matter how late she stayed up. While she didn't miss Dennis, she did miss her cube mates, who refused to believe that Leann might not have a life of bliss. Leann planted a larger garden but found she was uncomfortable on her knees pulling weeds, and by her third round of canning tomatoes, she knew it would take her years to use what she already canned. She gave some of the harvest away, and the rest of it spoiled. She prepared tomatoes in every way she could think of and ate only a small amount of what she'd grown. The basement space filled with Mason jars stacked higgly piggly. She intended to get the cans sorted but never seemed to find the time. It perplexed her that she still was so busy, although she couldn't quite figure out what she was doing to fill up her time.

Leann's retirement expectations clashed with its reality. She felt unmoored by the shift in daily rhythm. She switched from having two-thirds of her waking hours dictated by her job of forty years to having all of her waking hours available for whatever she wanted. Before retirement, she thought she'd feel like she was on an extended vacation. She didn't expect to feel lonely or adrift. The hobbies she never seemed to have time for before weren't as engaging as she thought they would be. It left her wondering what she was supposed to do with her time. She felt like she should know what she wanted at this time in her life, but the truth was she didn't. She wondered if maybe the best part of her life was over and she should just accept that she was now, well, old.

Transitions come in all varieties. They can be expected, like Leann's retirement, or unexpected, like Leann's discovery that her old hobbies no longer interested her. Transitions can be self-determined or forced by external factors. Here are just a few major life transitions:

- ❏ Getting your first job
- ❏ Graduating from high school

- ❑ Moving away from home
- ❑ Having your first serious relationship
- ❑ Getting married
- ❑ Having a baby
- ❑ Buying a house
- ❑ Having a parent die
- ❑ Changing careers
- ❑ Breaking up/getting divorced
- ❑ Becoming an empty nester
- ❑ Retiring from active working life
- ❑ Becoming a grandparent
- ❑ Getting remarried
- ❑ Being a caregiver for a loved one
- ❑ Experiencing a health crisis
- ❑ No longer being able to drive

Which transitions have you been through? What others you would add to the list?

Intentional vs. Haphazard Transitions

Regardless of whether you have experienced a planned transition or if one arrives unexpectedly, notice how you interact with that transition and determine how you feel about the change. You can be either active, what I call *intentional*, or passive, what I call *haphazard*, as you adjust to your life transition. My theory is that the life transitions that occur earlier in life are ones we engage in more intentionally because we are in the process of establishing ourselves or the well-being of someone else depends upon it. Conversely, the transitions that occur later in life may be more haphazard, meaning experienced more passively.

Life transitions often include a combination of planned and unplanned aspects. The impact of life transitions on your social community demonstrates this blend of planned and unplanned. While most people carefully save for financial well-being in retirement, how many consciously plan out what their social group will look like or anticipate that they may want to intentionally cultivate new friendships? Social dynamics also change after a divorce or when a spouse dies. Suddenly, you might be the only single person in a group of couples. Or you might move to a new city and feel intimidated by meeting new people. In each of these situations, you have the power to be passive or active, haphazard or intentional.

Having a child requires an intentional response to a life transition. You usually buy a lot of baby gear—a car seat, crib, stroller, high chair, diapers, wipes, onesies, pajamas, day clothes, blankets, bottles, books, developmental toys, and on and on. In addition to all the gear, there's a steep learning curve to care for a baby—not only do you want to keep him alive, but you want him to thrive. How much and when should he eat? Is he pooping enough and is it the right color? Why won't he sleep? How do I pack a diaper bag? There's a learning curve on self-care, too, especially for a new parent. How do you manage to care for this little one when your own sleep quotient isn't being met? How can you fit taking a shower into his schedule? What just happened to your body? The stakes to be successful as a parent are pretty high, so people invest a lot of intentional effort even when they cannot predict all aspects of the transition. They take it one issue at a time, and usually with intention.

Three concrete questions are useful during transitions: What skills are necessary? What stuff will you want? and Who can help you transition? Let's look at how that plays out for the life transition of having a baby.

What **skills** are necessary?
- ✓ Feeding baby through teen years
- ✓ Basic care
- ✓ Surviving on little sleep
- ✓ Nurturing growth
- ✓ Managing appointments
- ✓ Coordinating with other caregivers

What **stuff** will you want?
- ✓ A lot

Who can **help** you transition?
- ✓ Spouse, parent, sitter, friends, doctor, etc.

If you have children, I'm sure you could add to the lists above. Our purpose here is to demystify the process. The three components of skills, stuff, and help are ones to address in any life transition.

Now let's look at the life transition of having that child go to college, often referred to as creating an "empty nest." Because you aren't adding a new thing into your life, it can be easy to have this transition be more of a passive experience, meaning one that sneaks up on you without much preparation for the impact it will have on *you*. Yes, you have helped your child to consider, visit, and apply to colleges or to enter the workforce and move into her own apartment. You definitely experienced feelings of loss and anticipated loss at the thought of having them leave (or maybe excitement?). But did you intentionally consider how the tempo of your day might change without that additional person to cook for, care for, and interact with? Was your sense of purpose wholly centered on caring for that child or have you been slowly building other fulfilling activities? Have you considered a possible change of dynamic between you and your spouse?

Transitions like having an empty nest can easily be haphazard. You sort of realize the change is coming, but then it hits you, making you even more flustered because you're fighting the crisis as it happens. Here are clues to tell if your transition is haphazard:

- Did the situation just seem to happen? (anticipated or unanticipated)
- Are you having trouble accepting that it happened?
- Are your expectations of the change different than the reality?
- Are you isolating yourself and not reaching out for help?

We will focus more on the importance of acknowledging and accepting change in Section 3. For now, notice that these questions can help identify where and how you are responding to a transition.

The good news is that once you have acknowledged and accepted that a change has occurred, you can approach it with the same problem-solving method that is applied in intentional transitions. How might that look for the empty nest scenario?

What **skills** are necessary?

- ✓ Learning to help from a distance
- ✓ Getting used to a quieter home
- ✓ Interacting with your partner differently
- ✓ Re-evaluating how you spend your time
- ✓ Re-evaluating your purpose

What **stuff** will you want?

- ✓ Do you need to store kids' stuff? For how long?
- ✓ Will you use this space for something else?

Who can **help** you transition?

- ✓ Spouse, Friends, Counselor, etc.

If you focus only on what your child should do to prepare, you miss the preparation *you* must have. Not addressing your own transition leads to feeling out of alignment, out of sorts, and off track in life.

Magic Wand Exercise

Go get a pencil or pen. Close your eyes and imagine yourself as Cinderella's fairy godmother (or godfather). For now, feel the smooth cylinder of the pencil between your fingertips. Lift your hand, rotating your wrist in a circle three times to the right. Say "Bibbity, Bobbity, Boo!" Did you smile or laugh? Good. This mind frame connects you to the truest part of you that knows your own solutions.

- Now, close your eyes and think of what is most frustrating about your life right now. Got it? Write it down and tell your partner.

- If you could wave your magic wand to change that, what would be different?
- Spend a few moments with your eyes closed paying attention to what is different. What are you noticing?
- Who is there? Who is not there?
- What things are around you?

We're Off to See the Wizard

In case you didn't notice, this chapter's title alludes to the scene in *The Wizard of Oz* where Dorothy, Scarecrow, and Tin Man walk through the dark forest. They're afraid of what might be lurking in the trees. Out jumps Lion, who boasts and bullies them as they tremble with fear on the ground. Dorothy trembles, too, until Lion threatens her dog, Toto. Lion's attack on her dog prompts Dorothy to act courageously, swoop up Toto, and smack Lion's face. Suddenly, Lion's façade melts to reveal his own terrified state. Lion then sings a song identifying what he perceives as his main problem and what he believes will fix it. Dorothy invites him to join their hero's journey to see the Wizard, who will magically solve their problems by giving them the qualities that they think will make them successful. If you have seen the movie, you know that the Wizard (the outside entity) cannot give the characters what they seek; their solution lies in rediscovering the qualities that have existed inside of them all along.

You are more resilient and resourceful than you think. You have faced many life transitions already and gotten through them. You have problem-solved new situations using your fluid intelligence and built a solid crystallized intelligence. You have cultivated habits and methods that have served you well in the situations where they were needed. Likely, you have also established habits that aren't so functional. Even so, that doesn't undercut your ability to be the hero of your own story. Let's move forward now with the stories where you get to apply your expertise for someone else, practice the re-evaluation process, and examine where you might need to realign.

Discovery Questions

- Write a letter to yourself to read once you've completed this book. What do you hope to be clearer about? What do you hope to have completed?

CHAPTER 2

Kitchen Conundrum:

Cooking for a Big Family Turned Small

"It's not an empty nest until they get their stuff out of the basement."
An audience member at my downsizing presentation

Linda's Story

Linda hated throwing away food, yet week after week she found herself doing just that. When her four kids were still at home, it had been a challenge to keep them fed on a smaller budget. But Linda figured out how to do that by roasting meat on Sunday, then repurposing what was left over into other meals throughout the week. She spent hours clipping and organizing coupons and browsing store flyers. Once her kids were in high school and she returned to work, coupons became less important. At that point, convenience took priority. Shopping at Costco had been a saving grace for her hungry teens and their friends. Now a pan of lasagna for herself and her husband, David, lasted for days. By the second meal of leftovers, she felt like she couldn't choke down another bite.

When Linda opened her pantry, boxes perched precariously on top of cans that were lined into the dark reaches of the deep shelves. Cooking felt like a game of Jenga. Finding a can of green beans to make her famous casserole became a dangerous seek-and-find mission. So, she bought a flat of green beans to keep in the garage. It was easier to grab a can from the flat. Most of r food purchases from Costco began going into the garage, gradually crowding out David's ability to park inside. He felt a bit perturbed about having to park outside for the previous year. But since he wasn't the one cooking, Linda felt he should put up with it.

Her two youngest—twin girls—didn't eat quite as much in high school as their older brothers and they certainly didn't like left-overs. They told their mom to buy less and to make smaller meals, even buying her a couple of "Cooking for Two" cookbooks after they went to college. As much as their advice made logical sense to Linda, she didn't change her habits. It seemed easier to keep cooking in the way she was used to than to deal with new and complex recipes.

Pause & Notice

Slowing down to notice what is going on is one of the most undervalued aspects of behavior change. Until you stop racing through life, you won't increase your awareness and figure out what's causing chaos in your life. Noticing behaviors may not feel like an action, but it is *the* action to take before you can choose a different way. I've also included this section because of **Truth #1: People can see the situation more clearly with others than with themselves.** Let's practice those noticing skills with Linda's story.

- What problems does Linda see?
- What problems do others see?
- How many people did Linda cook for in the past? How many now?
- How was Linda successful in the past?
- What kinds of negative labels do you imagine Linda puts upon herself?

- What stands in the way of Linda doing things differently?
- What advice would you give Linda?

continuing old habits that aren't suitable

The Tipping Point

The purpose of this exercise is to articulate and build awareness of a person's beliefs about a situation from different angles. It takes the comparison of a pros and cons list and adds another dimension. Recall **Truth #2: People do not change until the pain of staying the same exceeds the pain of changing.** When individuals know they need to make a change, they typically focus on the pain of changing, are filled with feelings of dread, and then go into full-blown avoidance mode.

This exercise starts with filling out the Pain of Remaining the Same column—which may not have been fully examined before—then moves to the Pain of Changing column. Having these side by side lets you see which side of the decisional scale is heaviest. The third column, Benefits of Changing, adds another facet that may tip the scales towards change. The chart is based on the concepts found in Motivational Interviewing and the Stages of Change model. Motivation to change increases when the person filling out the form articulates ways to do things differently. If others insist on change, then that person will likely voice resistance to changing.

Let's look at how Linda might fill out the Tipping Point. Linda has identified some possible changes: to cook in smaller quantities, to stop buying in bulk, and to clear out the kitchen cabinets.

Linda's Tipping Point

PAIN OF REMAINING THE SAME	PAIN OF CHANGING	BENEFITS OF CHANGING
Wasting food	Learning a new way of cooking	Feeling proud of herself + opportunity to have fun learning a new approach
Wasting money	Getting used to shopping in a regular grocery store	Saving money
Choking down leftovers from big portions	Going thru cabinets and tossing more old food = facing mistakes	Following her value of not being wasteful
Having tension with husband over the garage	Facing her empty nest	Parking car in garage protects it and eases marital tension
Stressed by cooking when her cabinets are crowded		Being able to find ingredients easily in cabinets reduces stress
		Making food in smaller quantities means she enjoys it more
		Her husband can get involved too

Visualize Success

This exercise has two benefits. First, it defines concretely what a completed project will look like and feel like. Second, it encourages you to imagine yourself completing it. Research shows that your brain changes in a positive way when you see yourself successfully navigating the steps of a process.

It's important for Linda to imagine herself being successful in this process. Before she can imagine success, first she ought to define what success means for her. How will she know when she is successful? The answer could involve a physical measurement, such as her food fitting into her kitchen cabinets, or that cooking in smaller portions creates no leftovers. Her success could also be measured by how she feels or doesn't feel when she is in her kitchen or garage.

Remember **Truth #4: If you cannot imagine a better future, you will not step out of the past.** Linda must start identifying the possibilities of the present and future for her to register that things can be different and still feel good or even better.

What will success look like for Linda? What will success feel like?

- Success will look like having food fit into the kitchen cabinets and not be kept in other rooms. Success means being able to park the car in the garage.
- Success will feel like wanting to be in the kitchen. She won't feel so overwhelmed by the idea of cooking.

Project Action Plan

Let's put some of these pieces together in an action plan. Later, there will be an action plan specifically for habits. The Project Action Plan sets aside time to address the accumulation of things. I've designed these examples to demonstrate how a person and her helper might get through the stuff backlog and reorganize a space. There are other ways to approach these projects, but this is how I would start. Project and Habit Action Plans are based on **Truth #5: You need three things to be successful: a clear goal; a specific time/date to do it; and an accountability partner.** Notice how these are part of Linda's plan.

Linda's Project Action Plan

Goal: To have all the food contained in the kitchen.

What needs to be done: Go through all the food in the kitchen and garage.

What to do with it: Keep food that is not expired, that fits in the cabinet and that Linda will likely use; donate unexpired food that doesn't fit in the cabinet; and toss what is old or expired.

Where to start: The main pantry.

When: Saturday from 9 a.m. to 1 p.m.

Who: Even though Linda is mortified to have anyone else see her kitchen, she has hired a professional organizer to help her because she is so overwhelmed by the mess. Linda has not followed through organizing on her own and realizes she needs accountability. Also, she suspects that her husband or kids would make judgmental comments if they were helpers. Linda knows that it is torturous for her to physically throw away food, so having someone else do it eases her anxiety.

Over approximately two years, I earned the credential of Certified Professional Organizer in Chronic Disorganization® (CPO-CD®) through the Institute for Challenging Disorganization. Recertification is required every

three years. Another industry certification is Certified Professional Organizer®
(CPO®) through the National Association of Productivity and Organizing
Professionals℠. Not every organizer invests in his or her training to this
extent. A professional organizer's education is one aspect to evaluate when
finding a match for you.

Linda will:

- Predetermine amounts of cans/boxes from each food category;
- Place the kept items back into cabinets;
- Pack up food to be donated; and
- Take the donations tomorrow to the food pantry that her church runs.

The Organizer will:

- Pull food from the cabinets and garage;
- Check the expiration dates;
- Discard expired food and take those bags out to the garbage;
- Group unexpired food into like categories (canned vegetables, fruits, rice, etc.); and
- Help Linda estimate how much the food cabinets will hold.

When Zombies Attack

I stumbled on the Zombie Apocalypse test when I challenged myself and
others to eliminate an unused small kitchen appliance. My bread machine
hadn't been used in about three years and filled one-third of a cabinet. I had
mixed feelings about letting it go. While I didn't really use it, what if I needed it?

Because of the hint of uncertainty, my instinct was to stop the process and hold on to the bread maker. Instead, I leaned into my fears by writing them down, with a possible solution next to each line. My first fear was, "What if I want fresh bread?" Its solution was simple. I can easily get fresh bread from the grocery store bakery. Next was the worry, "What if I decide to become a pizza dough aficionado and want to use a bread maker?" I could solve this by buying one of the many donated bread makers from Goodwill.

My final fear was ridiculous. I felt silly even writing it down. I asked, "What if there's a zombie apocalypse and the only way I can get bread is to make it on my own?" I stared at this odd question for a moment. I didn't even know I had this irrational fear until I made my list. But there it was. My response to that problem was acknowledging that if zombies were on the loose, I would have problems more significant than fresh bread.

The purpose of this section is to write down all the fears—regardless of rationality. I know that the undead only exists in fiction. A fear doesn't have to make sense to influence how you behave. In fact, the scariest fears remind us that we aren't in control. By trying to deny that our fears exist, we close off discovering what we *can* do to recover from having them happen. My first and second examples had straight-forward solutions. A zombie attack did not have a solution, but it did provide a much-needed perspective. We dig deep in this section to uncover what fears may be lingering there and interfering with the change process.

Now that you've had a chance to analyze Linda's situation, let's look at some of the unexamined fears that may be influencing her behaviors. These are the kinds of issues that I might identify with a client during our work together. This section is based on **Truth #3: Unless people voice their worst fear, they will not make a change.** Linda might think that her issue centers on having time and energy to sort through her food. She's wrong about that though. Lurking just below the surface are two huge monsters that have to do with who she thinks she should be as a person. The first involves the error of overbuying and misspending money. The second rejects being a "wasteful person" who throws away food. Let's look at these individually.

Money Mistakes

Have you ever made a mistake? Yep, me, too. Every person on Earth has made mistakes, and they continue to do so daily. Linda wants to be a person who doesn't make mistakes. Do you see the trap here?

Most of us strive for excellence. Achieving excellence is not the same as trying to be perfect. When you aim for excellence, you can make mistakes and learn from them. With perfection, your mistakes indicate that you are a flawed and unworthy person. These two mindsets tell opposing stories about what makes someone successful. I appreciate Brené Brown's research on feeling shame vs. feeling guilt and how people respond to mistakes within each context. All of her books are thought-provoking and useful; however, if you aren't a big reader, you can watch her TED Talks on YouTube. Reading her books has transformed the way I respond to making mistakes. In *Daring Greatly: How the Courage to Be Vulnerable Transforms the Way We Live, Love, Parent, and Lead*, Brown distinguishes between having a response of shame or of guilt:

Shame is a focus on self, guilt is a focus on behavior. Shame is "I am bad." Guilt is "I did something bad." How many of you, if you did something that was hurtful to me, would be willing to say, "I'm sorry. I made a mistake?" How many of you would be willing to say that? Guilt: I'm sorry. I made a mistake. Shame: I'm sorry. I am a mistake.

Did you catch the difference? Guilt means you *did* something wrong. Shame means you *are* wrong. If Linda feels shame in response to throwing away large quantities of expired food, she convicts herself for being a bad person. People with a shame mindset use all sorts of denial tactics to avoid facing a mistake. It's easy to see why: the verdict cannot get much more damning than being a defective human being. By contrast, if Linda's mindset is guilt, she will still wish she hadn't overbought, but she can separate the behavior of overbuying from her value as a whole person. Shame thrives when it is unexamined and unspoken; it runs your life—your decisions, sense of self, and relationships. It's essential to voice feelings of shame because then you can begin to shed light on it. Shame loses power over you when you bring it into the light. You can begin to detach yourself from the thought and test out whether or not it's true.

Moving from a shame mindset to a guilt mindset requires you to develop self-compassion. Self-compassion is when you treat yourself with the same kindness with which you treat your friends. Let's say Linda's friend had overbought food. What might Linda say to her? She would probably say things like, "It's no big deal" or "You can't change the past, but you can change what you do in the future," or "We all make mistakes." You can practice shifting out of a shame mindset by imagining that a friend has done what you did. Identify how you would treat her and apply that kindness to yourself.

When it comes to processing guilt for your behavioral mistakes, the best approach is to admit your error, forgive yourself, and identify an alternate behavior for the future. Here's the forgiveness formula:

I made a mistake by _____.
Everyone makes mistakes, and so do I.
I forgive myself for _____.
Next time, I will do this instead: _____.

Using this formula, Linda can acknowledge her buying mistakes and choose differently in the future. The project helper may act as a witness to and advocate for Linda's emerging self-compassion. With practice, Linda can learn that her behavioral mistakes do not cancel out the many positive aspects of her character.

Being a Wasteful Person

Closely tied to feeling defective for making money mistakes is the association between throwing away useful but unwanted items and being a wicked, wasteful person. Anyone who has grown up in a family with few resources or who had parents who lived during the Great Depression knows that being wasteful could mean the difference between eating and not eating, or getting by versus going without. Someone with few resources must become resourceful.

My husband's grandfather, Glenn, was born in 1920. He explained how his mother bought chicken feed bags by the pattern on the bag and sewed them into dresses. As the dresses wore out, they were made into bloomers. "Handed down clothes were common in families or among neighbors," said Glenn, "if any wear was left, the philosophy was not to throw it away, but to share it." One of the biggest resources for Glenn and his family was their garden. Produce could be traded or given to others. Members of the community looked out for one another, said Glenn: "We were all in the same boat with no money when the 1929 crash happened and banks closed." The garden also provided enough food for later because "Mother canned any and all produce so we had shelves of vegetables—canned fresh from the garden— plus grapes, cherries, asparagus, rhubarb, horseradish, potatoes by the bushel, and onions. We were never hungry." At a time when many people suffered from a scarcity of belongings, what was not scarce in Glenn's childhood was his feeling of belonging. "We lived the good life," he said. "We loved each other and were happy to be a family."

Having grown up on a farm myself, I experienced the sense of teamwork a family feels when they must work together to succeed. Although I wasn't often a happy participant in farm chores, I did benefit from the fresh food-to-table way of eating. I learned how to be resourceful with what was available, and developed a strong work ethic. While our faster-paced world has many benefits, convenience foods, which are packed with additives and preservatives, have reduced our health; additional packaging adds to landfills; and busy families are often pulled in many different directions rather than united as a family team working together for survival. Today, families face different challenges in reference to their belongings due to widely available, inexpensive products.

The value of not being wasteful became ingrained in how the Greatest Generation, who lived through the Great Depression, did things and raised their children. Members of the Greatest Generation might rewash plastic baggies, reuse tin foil, and save bits of string. The Greatest Generation raised Baby Boomers, who may or may not exhibit the values of frugality, but who definitely felt the guilt attached to throwing something away. Baby Boomer's kids, Gen X, got a toned-down version of the value of "waste not, want not" and Gen Xer's kids, Millennials, seem relatively removed from the idea that it is a sin (a character flaw, unforgivable error) to throw someone away that could still be consumed.

How could attitudes have changed so much in four generations and less than 100 years? Both the Greatest Generation and Millennials created appropriate reactions to the conditions of their environment. In the 1920s, goods were hard to come by, cost a lot and were made to be repaired. In 2019, goods are plentiful, cheap, and made to be replaced. Why wouldn't someone in the Great Depression save pieces of string? Why wouldn't Millennials throw away a piece of string that can be easily and cheaply replaced? A Millennial doesn't place as high a value on a piece of furniture being made to last for generations; they'd rather have a stylish design—however cheaply made— than something bulky, brown, but build to last. Life in the 2010s didn't involve fancy sets of china and silver-plated utensils. In the 1920s, these items were highly-valued treasures to be passed from generation to generation. So you see that each generation responds to their environments, which are quite different.

This isn't the place to argue the points of one generation's approach over another, because there are good and bad aspects of each. It is the place to recognize that being a "wasteful person" is a concept that doesn't necessarily exist in every generation.

Linda's pattern was cooking too much food for two people, eating some of the leftovers, and then keeping the rest in the back of the fridge until it became moldy. To change any of these habits was uncomfortable, and when she felt discomfort, she perceived it as a sign that she should step back from doing things differently and step towards what felt normal. Linda could try to use willpower to change, but she won't be successful until she learns the skills to manage her discomfort.

Linda, a Baby Boomer, raised by someone who was a teen during the Great Depression, had a lot of unexamined beliefs about being wasteful. Although she did not rewash her food storage bags, she did save take-out containers to reuse, and she had a lot of trouble managing leftovers. Linda adopted the belief that throwing away leftovers that were not yet fuzzy with mold meant that she was a terrible person. If she delayed discarding leftovers long enough for mold to grow, she gave herself permission to discard them due to the health risk.

Linda created her own set of rules to accommodate the rules about wastefulness set up by her parents. Linda's decision-making process entailed mostly unexamined assumptions about food waste, which will undermine her habit changes until she brings the unconscious beliefs into the light and chooses what food rules make the most sense for her right now.

Changing Habits

The first step to change habits is to look at what belief(s) might be reinforcing a behavior. Linda could make a list of what rules about leftovers she has created. She may realize that she has not allowed herself to throw away leftovers before they mold. If she has a helper on her self-examination journey (which I highly recommend), that person might ask, "Who made this rule?" and "What makes this a valuable or not valuable rule?" I'm guessing that Linda has never considered these questions. Linda may have metaphorical light bulb appear over her head when it dawns on her that she has permission to make different rules about food. The helper should write these new rules down. Linda may feel energized with the further realization that she doesn't have to feel guilty about throwing away extra food if she cooks less food to begin with. The helper can help her brainstorm ideas of how to cook less.

Want to know a secret about changing behaviors? Hint: it's impossible to just stop doing the unwanted behavior. Try not to think of a pink elephant when I say not to think of a pink elephant. Your focus is on not doing the thing you are used to doing, which means your attention is still on the unwanted habit. You must replace the unwanted habit with a different one so that your focus is on doing the new thing rather than not doing the old thing. Instead of focusing on not drinking diet soda, focus on drinking water with lemon. Instead of making a large pan of lasagna and eating it all at once, make the full recipe and split it into four servings, three of which get frozen for future use.

Successful change will be more likely if you look at the beliefs that may be driving your behavior, decide whether those beliefs fit your situation or are carryovers from someone else, create your own rules, and focus on the replacement behavior (not on avoiding your old habit). Let's see how that might look for Linda in her habit action plan.

Linda's Habit Action Plan

What needs to be done: Learn how to cook in smaller quantities.

What to do with it:

- Sign up for a "cooking for two" class with her husband at a local restaurant;
- Identify her favorite family recipes to organize into an expandable file;
- Reduce her cookbook collection;
- Post a reminder above her stove that says "Cooking for two is fun to do;"
- Take a photo of that reminder to use as a screen saver for the next month;
- Cancel her Costco membership, or, at least avoid shopping there for the next three months;
- Shop at a regular grocery buy only what's on her list; and
- Consider using a grocery delivery service.

Where to start: Cookbooks and Recipes.

When: Saturday from 9 a.m. to 1 p.m.

Who: Linda was so pleased with how much easier the process was by hiring a professional organizer that she booked another appointment. This time, they would cull her recipes and cookbooks. Working with paper is something Linda would otherwise avoid, so the accountability was essential. The organizer presorted items to make it easier for Linda to make decisions. If Linda were doing this on her own, she would have to switch between figuring out what categories the items fit into and deciding on whether she needs them. For some people, this attention shift is so exhausting that it undermines progress.

Linda will:

- Page through the cookbooks that look more well-used to find favorite family recipes and either tear it out of the cookbook or keep the cookbook;
- Find favorite recipes among the loose recipes;
- Be realistic about not using those 1980s cookbooks on wok cooking, church cookbooks, and the many cookbooks she has not opened in years;
- Create the reminders in her kitchen and on her phone;
- Sign up for a cooking class; and
- Make a plan for grocery shopping, perhaps by signing up for grocery delivery.

The Organizer will:

- Help Linda identify what cooking for two might look like as far as the number of weekly meals: new recipes; tried and true recipes reduced in size; and convenience or restaurant meals;

- Pull cookbooks from the shelves and sort into three categories: cookbooks that appear more highly used, outdated cookbooks that appear unused, recent cookbooks that appear unused;
- Presort loose recipes into categories for Linda to decide on;
- Set up the expandable file: label categories, and file favorites;
- Remind Linda to create her reminders; and
- If needed, assist in finding and signing up for a cooking class or learning how to use a grocery delivery service.

Your Turn: Pause & Notice

It is time for you to slow down and look at your own habits around cooking. What do you notice about yourself? Be honest about your current habits. If you find yourself wanting to write down what you wish you were doing, do that to the side of your truthful answer.

- How many people do you currently cook for?
- How many nights a week do you make dinner?
- How many nights a week do you eat out?
- What from Linda's story resonated with you?
- What action steps will you take around cooking? Your kitchen in general?

Take a Photo

Increase your commitment to change by taking photographs of the areas you will work on. Photos help you see your environment in an unbiased way. It's easy to become blind to what your space actually looks like when you live in it. If you live with someone who struggles to see the space objectively, take a photo and show them, but don't be a jerk about it. This technique isn't meant to convince someone how wrong they are; the purpose is to raise consciousness. Also, taking photos creates a "before" version to compare to your "after" version. We may think we'll remember the original mess, but often we don't. Having proof provides a wonderful sense of accomplishment.

Take a photo of your kitchen and inside the cabinets that frustrate you.

How to Complete "Your Tipping Point"

First identify the negative consequences associated with staying the same in the Pain of Remaining the Same column (e.g., can't use the room, feeling like a failure, can't put the house up for sale). Another way to brainstorm things for the pain of remaining the same column is to answer the question: "If I could wave a magic wand, what would I take away?"

Be as specific in describing its adverse effects on:

- your home environment
- your finances
- your feelings about yourself
- your relationships
- and your health

Next, think of reasons why you don't want to change for the Pain of Changing column (e.g., is it too much effort? Do you know how? Do you have the support you need? Are you avoiding certain emotions?) Consider what might contribute to your resistance. Sometimes a person's behavior is driven by being comforted by the familiar, even when the familiar isn't healthy. Be alert to the intensity of these responses, as it may signal you have deeper emotional work to address via therapy. If that's the case, give yourself the gift of addressing this with the appropriate resource.

Finally, fill in the Benefits of Changing column. You can either look at the first column and note the opposite or find answers by finishing the sentence: "It would be such a relief to..."

There's no need to have the vertical columns match across the grid. Just come up with a list for each column and add to it as needed. You will know you are on track if you begin to have "ah-ha!" moments during and after completing it. Push yourself to fill as many boxes in each column as possible. You are likely to discover previously unknown reasons you have been stuck and to reinforce your desires to change, thereby pushing you over the tipping point of the decisional scale towards action.

PAIN OF REMAINING THE SAME	PAIN OF CHANGING	BENEFITS OF CHANGING

How to Complete "Visualize Your Success"

Fuzzy goals don't get specific on details. How can you know you are done if you haven't defined what done looks like? "Clean up the office" is a fuzzy goal. "Reduce sixty books to forty" or "shred bills older than 2012" are specific and measurable. You know you are done when you have gotten to forty books or eliminated the old bills. Also, get specific with your interior feelings of being done. Instead of the fuzzy "I'll feel good," be precise with "I'll feel calm when I see open space on my bookshelf" or "I won't feel stressed every time I open my file drawer."

Have you heard the phrase, "Whether you think you can or can't, you are right"? When you see yourself as being incapable of a reasonable goal, you will undermine yourself every time. Fully imagining yourself completing the actions and arriving at the end attunes your brain to success. Try it and see how much easier it is to follow through.

Visualize Your Success

What will success look like for you? What will success feel like?

How to Complete "Your Project Action Plan"

Linda's Project Action Plan modeled how valuable getting specific can be. Continuing the theme of getting fuzzy goals to come into focus, this plan helps you determine what area you are working on, what your rules are for keeping and discarding, and where you will start. Also, you set a specific time to work and identify who will support you. I cannot emphasize enough the importance of a supportive helper or paid expert. You will gain accountability to show up, be anchored to the task by the other person's presence, have another set of hands, and benefit from his or her compassionate assistance. Haven't you tried to do it alone enough times?

The other part of the project plan is to assign tasks to different people and to plan smaller steps in the process. Not everyone can break a big project into doable parts. Ideally, your chosen helper is able to take what feels overwhelming to you and keep the plan moving. Brainstorm parts of the project on a blank piece of paper, and then list steps within each part until you find your next step. If that next step feels overwhelming, keep making it smaller until you think, "I can do that!" It's okay to have your first step be something as basic as "Pull everything out of the drawer." You may decide to just see how it goes as far as who does what. In that case, there's value in reflecting on how things went after the fact because you may discover what to do differently next time or unlock a recipe for success that can be duplicated in other areas.

Your Project Action Plan

What needs to be done:

What to do with it:

Where to start:

When:

Who:

You will:

The helper will:

How to Complete "Your Habit Action Plan"

You may have realized by this point that getting belongings organized represents only one piece of the process. Another important step which will reinforce maintaining your space or new system is to examine your habits. Take time to answer the question, "What habits got this space looking so chaotic?"

Once you have articulated these habits, consider which behavior you want to replace with a new habit. Similar to the process of the Project Action Plan, you want to be specific with what habit you are targeting, what are the new guidelines for your behavior, and what your first experiment will be. Stop the fuzziness by setting a time and day to tackle the habit and determining what will support you. It may be a person physically next to you, a person whom you call, a product such as a timer, phone app, or even a notecard posted in the area.

Write out the steps you will take to do things differently, then pay attention to how your habit experiment goes. In what areas are you getting stuck? Can you adjust your habit by reducing a few steps or enlisting other people? Your long-term success depends on your awareness of how these habit experiments are working out and your willingness to be flexible (not rigid) with adjusting the steps and expectations.

Your Habit Action Plan

What needs to be done:

What to do with it:

Where to start:

When:

Who:

You will:

The helper will:

Now that I have introduced and explained how to complete your version of the exercises, they will not be included in future chapters. Instead, go to https://www.greenlightorganizing.com/workbook/ to download a free companion workbook that will be easier to write on (and not upset the perfectionists among us who prefer not to journal directly into a print book).

The Purpose of Discovery Questions

Journaling can be a powerful tool for self-discovery. The Discovery Questions at the end of each chapter should not be skipped if you want to find out who you are now. You'll notice that many of them look to the past. What does that have to do with now? The answer is, more than you realize. Take time to explore these discovery questions and trust the process I have designed. You'll be glad you did.

Discovery Questions

- What do you think of when you hear the word "home"?
- Where have you lived that felt the most like home? The least like home?
- What was life like after your children moved out? If this doesn't apply to you, write about where you lived after you left your parent's house.

CHAPTER 3

Paper, Paper, Everywhere

"Every piece of paper represents a decision that hasn't been made,
or an action that hasn't be taken."
A wise attendee of my class

Patricia's Story

Patricia loves learning about health topics, decorating, gardening, and psychology—pretty much everything. Two decades ago, she bought a beautiful four-drawer wooden file cabinet, in which she created files for each subject that interested her. Every clipped article was sorted in alphabetized files to be easily accessible. She helped her friends out of many dilemmas by providing advice or information about a variety of subjects. Although she never had children of her own, she had a close-knit relationship with her nephews and nieces, marking birthdays and other special days with cards.

Patricia led an active life in retirement. She belonged to a retired teachers' group, the church women's group, and a book club that she leads. She occasionally tutors and she reads a lot. In addition to her city's newspaper, she receives the *New York Times* and subscribes to seven different magazines. In recent years, her magazine reading has gotten backlogged. At first, she bought magazine files and labeled her collections by year. Lately, the magazines are piling up near her bookcase, and some are still in the plastic sleeve they were mailed in.

A large pile of clipped articles awaited filing or being mailed. Patricia's desktop computer and printer helped in printing out interesting articles she found online. She felt somewhat comfortable using the internet. Sometimes information disappeared, or warning messages appeared that she didn't know how to deal with, but she did the best she could and was more computer-savvy than some of her friends. Her newspaper reading really fell off since she began using her computer more. She liked the ritual of going through the printed pages, but often the news articles were already familiar to her from online articles posted on her computer home page.

The piles of magazines, newspapers, catalogs, newsletters, and clippings in her office, living room, and bedside were preventing her from having her groups to her house. This had never been a problem before. She even had a fight with her sister over the paper. Patricia had sent her niece a series of articles on the drawbacks of living with a boyfriend before marriage.

Patricia's sister called to say some pretty hurtful things after her daughter received the clippings, "No one wants your stupid articles anyway! They're just clutter. It's not the 1900s anymore. People don't cut out articles!"

Patricia felt devastated. She was only trying to be helpful and didn't want to see her precious niece get in a bad situation.

With all of this drama, Patricia felt out of sorts, yet she couldn't imagine getting rid of any of her paper. What if she missed out on some important piece of information? And wasn't it her right to state her opinion? She just wanted to share information.

Pause & Notice

- What problems does Patricia see?

- What problems do others see?

- How did reading and clipping articles benefit Patricia in the past?

- What stands in the way of Patricia doing things differently?

- What advice would you give Patricia?

The Tipping Point

PAIN OF REMAINING THE SAME	PAIN OF CHANGING	BENEFITS OF CHANGING
Piles of unread material in three rooms	Time reading what is unread or (gasp) recycling them without reading	Having a clearer house so she can host friends and groups
Piles of clipped articles to file	Time to file the articles	Feeling free of the guilt that she has to clip and file
Piles of clipped articles to mail	Being disconnected from family and friends to whom she mails articles	More time to connect with them by phone, email or in person
Always feeling behind and messy	Giving up her article clipping habit of many years will feel odd	Using the internet keeps info always accessible and reduces paper clutter
Not having friends over		Caught up on reading

Visualize Success

- Success will look like not having paper piles in her living room so she can host an event.
- Success will feel like the freedom of not being behind on going through magazines and newspapers or on writing notes and mailing the articles.

Patricia's Project Action Plan

Goal: to get rid of her paper piles so she can have friends over.

What needs to be done: Go through her piles of clipped articles and unread magazines and newspapers.

What to do with it: Recycle what she hasn't read and decide what to file.

Where to start: Her living room.

When: Monday from 9-11 a.m.

Who: Patricia described her problem to her book club friend, Susan. Patricia liked Susan because they shared a love of reading and learning. Susan was very organized herself, but she had other important qualities: she was a good listener and was not bossy. Patricia decided to take the risk of having Susan help her with the papers in her living room. If things didn't go well, then she would try a different approach.

Patricia will:

- Allow Susan to recycle the older newspapers and magazines without later retrieving them back from recycling;
- Acknowledge that she may feel uncomfortable, but trust that she will be okay;

- Create files for each category of clipped articles; and
- Place files into her file drawer without trying to incorporate the new and old files.

Susan will:

- Recycle any newspapers older than the current week and any magazines more than two months old, as decided by Patricia;
- Presort the articles by category; and
- Acknowledge that Patricia is taking a big step by recycling the unread material, follow the direction given by Patricia, and not give unsolicited advice or make judgmental comments.

When Zombies Attack

Baby Steps Are a Great Start

As an observer, you may think that the wisest action plan for Patricia would be to recycle all her clippings and magazines/newspapers. While this certainly was an option, such a big step would be too daunting for some people. By keeping her filing system intact for the time being and keeping a defined quantity of back issues, Patricia would begin to develop her "letting go muscles."

In addition to learning to let go of her backlog slowly, Patricia could get a better sense of how much she was actually able to read over a week or month. As time passes, Patricia would realize that she was getting behind again. New magazines and newspapers would arrive. Her amount of reading time would likely remain the same. The difference between those two factors would become apparent by the way that the piles quickly regenerated.

At that point, Patricia could do some math. How long did it take her to read through each magazine and newspaper? In a month, Patricia received seven magazines that took an average of two hours to read, totaling fourteen hours. She received sixty newspaper issues, which she read in around an hour each, totaling sixty hours. Overall, she had seventy-four hours of reading at an average of eighteen and a half hours per week. And that didn't even count what she read online, or the time she spent to clip the articles and file or mail them! Did Patricia realize that she had assigned herself the equivalent of a part-time job? It was easy to see how Patricia would feel burdened by her monthly reading regiment, let alone the burden of trying to get through that huge backlog.

By working in small sessions with Susan, Patricia could begin to notice aspects that she was too overwhelmed to process before. Not only are baby steps normal, but they are healthier in the long run. Patricia didn't have to have her file cabinet cleaned out before she could enjoy hosting her book club. The reward of connecting would boost her motivation to continue to do things differently. Clearing the file cabinet of the clipped articles she never refers to would be a project for a later time.

But My Collection Might Be Valuable!

Let's say that within Patricia's magazine piles was a complete collection of *People Magazine* from 1985-1995. Patricia took a lot of time to place these magazines into magazine holders. Each year fit nicely into three labeled binders. Her collection was complete and in order. It didn't matter that she hadn't opened the binders to look back at them. Patricia was proud because they showed how organized she was in that particular area for those ten years.

Many people get stuck on saving collections—even ones that are literally just taking up space and not being used—by telling themselves the following things:

- ❑ I can't reduce a collection. I'll either keep it all or give it all away.
- ❑ I took so much time to put it together that I am going to keep it for now.
- ❑ When I have more time, I will look through them again. There were some good articles in those pages.
- ❑ That collection is worth good money! What if I threw it away and found out I could have made a bunch of money selling it.
- ❑ But I have ALL the magazines. I can't just throw them away! Maybe I should bring them to a school, and the kids can use them for art projects or to a nursing home, and people can look through them.

It's much easier in the short term simply to keep something rather than investigate whether justifications about it are true. While it used to be more difficult to know the current market value for items, now the answers lie at the tip of your fingers. The auction and selling website, eBay, has been around since 1995. Its popularity has increased as brick and mortar antique stores have declined. The advantages of eBay are that it reaches a global audience, making the buying and selling experience feel relatively easy. While eBay has more competition with other selling sites than it used to, in general, it can still be considered a good gauge of market value for items.

Here's how you can check what an item's value is right now. Go to www.ebay.com. Type your item into the search bar. On the desktop version, look on the left side of the screen and scroll down until you see the filter "sold items" then click on that. The search will automatically reset to show items that have sold, showing the price and how much shipping cost. On the mobile version, click "filters," scroll down to click "sold items," and then click "done" at the upper right-hand corner to reset the search results. Similar to an in-person yard sale, a seller list an item at whatever price he wants. That doesn't mean someone will buy it. By using the filter of sold items, you can see what people are actually paying for items like yours. Shipping and handling should be figured into the price, too.

Patricia saw that someone sold for ten dollars and free shipping a group of four 1985 *People Magazines* where the singer Madonna appeared on the cover. This seller won't profit ten dollars because he had to pay to ship the magazine to the buyer. The seller also paid from each sale a percentage to eBay and to PayPal. In the end, this seller would profit less than two dollars a magazine for his effort. Patricia can decide if her time listing it, monitoring the listing, and preparing the magazines to ship justifies the effort. Perhaps a highly sought-after magazine issue *would* be worth the trouble. By searching on eBay, she can gain a sense of value. Whether that news is exhilarating or disappointing, at least it is information.

FOMO

Have you heard the phrase "Fear of Missing Out" or FOMO? This anxiety inducer stems from the belief that by not reading something you might miss out on some crucial information, like, what if honeybees are going extinct and the only way to save them is for every household in the state to build a bee watering system? How can you live with the guilt of killing off bees by not being informed? How will you help your friend solve her diabetes problem without the article on "10 diabetes-friendly recipes?" Your thinking seems more rational when you don't examine it too closely, when it may be more irrational than you realize.

Here's the thing about magazines and newspapers: they exist to sell advertising. Sure, they convey information. Occasionally, the info is life-altering. Most of the time, though, articles cover the same subjects and regurgitate the same basic tips. I bet you can recite the top five headlines on most women's magazines: *Lose Weight! Get Organized! Find Love! Look Younger!* and *Admire This Famous Person!*

Magazines would not exist if you felt confident about yourself. It is their job to continuously make you feel inadequate. Otherwise, you would stop buying the products in the ads and stop worrying that the articles might contain magical advice. The titles of online articles are set up this way, too.

I used to be a hapless victim to media. Then I noticed that the articles month-to-month weren't really unique. I realized I could just type in my problem into the Google search box and get thousands (or millions) of results. My teens know this. At their age, I had to rely on encyclopedias, magazines, newspapers, and books for information. Now they just type keywords into

YouTube and find an instructional video on how to braid hair a certain way or teach themselves to play guitar.

Just as my kids know no different than to use the internet, I knew no different than to find information the way I was taught. Information sources were rarer and more revered when I was a kid. To be published was an unusual accomplishment because the gatekeeper editors funneled out many voices. Now the system is diffuse, multi-voiced, with few gatekeepers. Information is not scarce. Discernment is the skill we most need to be taught, such as asking the key question, "Is this a good source of information?" In this day and age, you are less at risk of missing out on information and more at risk of getting bad information.

Believing that information is readily available on the internet and then knowing how to access it is the key to overcoming this zombie scenario. So, change your mindset and gather new skills. Let's see how Patricia might tackle changing her magazine clipping habit and let go of the files she never looks at.

Patricia's Habit Action Plan

What needs to be done: Stop clipping articles.

What to do with it: Experiment with resisting her urge to clip.

Where to start: This month's magazines.

When: Lunchtime each day this week.

Who: Patricia will spend each day at lunch reading her magazine, but not cutting out anything. She will mark the article with a Post-It note if she feels a strong urge to clip it. At the end of the week, Patricia will meet Susan for lunch at a cafe. Patricia will bring the magazines and discuss how the week went, with the option of discarding the magazines at the end of their lunch date.

Patricia will:

- Read her magazines each day without clipping articles;
- Notice how anxious she feels on a scale of 1-10, one being low and ten being the highest anxiety;
- When she feels compelled to clip an article, she will instead place a Post-it on that page indicating the number representing her anxiety level; and
- Be open to growing her letting go muscles.

Susan will:

- Praise Patricia for being willing to do an experiment;
- Express curiosity about Patricia's experiment by asking open-ended questions like, "What was it like to...;"
- Ask Patricia if she would be able to find the information in the articles she flagged again;
- Encourage Patricia to be brave and recycle the magazines; and
- Check in with Patricia in two days to see how Patricia feels about the experiment.

Your Turn: Pause & Notice

It's time to assess your own media collection. (Don't worry about including books because those have a whole chapter later.)

- How many print magazines and newspapers do you have?

- How long does it take you to read each magazine? Newspaper?

- How many hours per week do you need to read to keep up with that quantity?

- What from Patricia's story resonated with you?

- What action steps will you take with magazines and newspapers? Saving paper in general?

Take a photo of any piles of magazines and newspapers, magazine collections, catalogs, newsletters, etc.

Discovery Questions

- What advice would you give to a young person graduating from high school this year?

- If you could write a letter to yourself at 18, what would you say?

CHAPTER 4

Bad Math in the Bath

"You can never get enough of what you don't really need."
April Benson

Joan's Story

Joan never met a sale she didn't like: BOGO, BOGO 50%, Scratch Off to Reveal Your % Savings, Best Sale of the Season, and Senior Discount Day at Goodwill. "Only stupid people pay full price" was Joan's philosophy. She shopped year-round for Christmas and birthday gifts rather than wait until the last minute. She loved the thrill the hunt! Joan even had a list of what was the best month to buy which products.

Since her divorce fifteen years earlier, she had been forced to pinch pennies to buy things for her and her (then) high school aged daughter, Savannah. They got by, barely. Her ex-husband paid child support more or less on time, but he hated it and his second wife hated it even more. Joan got herself back into the workforce. Thank goodness she got a job because she had so much debt. She didn't think she would ever be able to retire.

Joan's daughter and two grandchildren lived two states away. She wished she could see them more often. To stay connected, Joan sent little presents to them every couple of months. She had quite a collection of possible gifts for her grandbabies. Everywhere she shopped, she saw fun things to give to them and Savannah.

Savannah's old bedroom was where Joan stored her stockpile. Gifts for any occasion could be found there: graduation, baby gift, wedding shower, birthday for him, birthday for her, friendship, and just because. The best gifts to get on sale were ones that everyone liked: candles and lotion. Joan felt a little embarrassed that the room had filled up. Savannah and her kids had to sleep on air mattresses when they visited, which seemed to be less and less. At Christmas, Joan overheard Savannah tell her youngest that they couldn't sleep on real beds because "Grammy can't stop buying things." The comment made her angry, and she decided to stop sending gifts to them throughout the year.

Joan liked bath products and candles herself. She knew what day in November she could get the lowest price on big candles at her favorite store. She always bought at least two flats worth. Whenever she shopped there throughout the year, she made sure to use her "Buy 3 get 1 free" coupons. New bath scents were so fun to try. Her bathroom cabinets were crammed full of her favorites. She had begun to store her extra personal supply in the gift stockpile. Sometimes the accumulation felt like too much. But how could she not take advantage of such good pricing?

Pause & Notice

- What problems does Joan see?
- What problems do others see?
- How did buying ahead benefit Joan in the past?
- What stands in the way of Joan doing things differently?
- What advice would you give Joan?

Joan's Tipping Point

PAIN OF REMAINING THE SAME	PAIN OF CHANGING	BENEFITS OF CHANGING
Gift room will continue to fill	Having to stop buying gifts	Saving money
Knowing at some level that she has too much stuff	Facing her spending mistakes	Feeling more financially responsible
Having no room for her family to stay	Paring down her stockpile	Having a place for her family to stay
Further separating from her daughter and grandchildren	Directly communicating her hurt feelings to her daughter	Becoming closer to her family
Continuing to go into debt	Having no replacement activity for shopping	Retiring earlier
Feeling like her family disapproves of her		
Having to work longer		

Visualize Success

- Success would look like getting the bed cleared and the gifts organized and accessible.

- Success would feel like the satisfaction of completing a project, a sense of calm when she walks into the room, ease in finding and giving gifts, and the happiness of hosting her daughter and grandkids.

Joan's Project Action Plan

Goal: To make it possible for Savannah and her grandkids to sleep in the gift room.

What needs to be done: Reduce the amount of the gift stockpile to what can fit in the closet and be easily accessible.

What to do with it: Organize the keep pile and find a donation option for the rest.

Where to start: With the stuff that is currently in the closet.

When: Tuesday at 10 a.m.

Who: Joan and a professional organizer with life coach training.

I earned my certification as a Certified Organizer Coach® (COC®) throughout many months through the Coach Approach for Organizer™. I'm required to recertify this credential every three years. Look for life coaches who have invested in quality training and who continue to improve their skills. See the Resources at the back of the book for a link to COCs in your area.

Joan will:
- Make decisions on her own items from the closet;
- Get clarification from Savannah on what can be thrown away (e.g., high school homework and worksheets);
- Honor Savannah's wishes of what to keep or not keep;
- Text Savannah photos of bigger items for her to decide on as they go;
- Dust and vacuum the newly cleared closet; and
- Explain to the organizer-coach what her gift-giving process is and what categories or recipients have bigger quantities.

The Organizer-Coach will:

- Carry the items from the closet into the family room;
- Box up Savannah's small childhood items for Savannah to look at during her next visit;
- Ask questions to elicit Joan's goals and help her engage in how her daughter's goals and hers are similar or different;
- Encourage Joan to take steps that create what she really wants;
- Help Joan take items to donation, if Joan wishes, and take out the trash/recycling;
- Stack the boxes for Savannah in a corner of Savannah's room; and
- Measure the closet and help Joan plan her gift closet space.

For their follow-up appointment, the organizer-coach purchased containers to go in the closet for Joan's gift bags, wrap, and other wrapping supplies. They began sorting by gift categories. Before that appointment, Joan agreed to make a list of who she buys gifts for during the year and how many general gifts she wants to have on-hand.

When Zombies Attack

Tipping the Scales towards Change

On the surface, it seemed as though Joan's problem was having a messy room. While there were external shifts that could be made, the bigger challenge was discovering what purpose shopping had for Joan. External things piled up because the underlying issues had been avoided. The interchange of buying objects was much simpler than interacting with loved ones. Things don't talk back, have expectations and feelings, or opinions and unpredictable reactions. What might have started as a hobby, or something to do that's interesting, had snowballed into a bigger problem.

Joan's desire to buy things to let her family know she loved them and was thinking of them reflected good intentions. On some level, Joan knew that her buying had gotten out of her control. She hadn't fully realized how badly until she overheard her granddaughter's comments. After some of the hurt feelings passed, Joan could step back from the gift room and really see how much was in there. It felt chaotic. She felt ashamed that she didn't have her house more together as an example for her grandkids.

As Thanksgiving approached, Joan's friend, Martha, asked about Joan's holiday plans. The whole story spilled out. Martha reminded Joan about the counselor who Joan saw during her divorce, wondering whether she had retired. They looked it up online and discovered that she was still in practice. Martha encouraged Joan to make a call right then. She phoned and left a message.

We all could use friends like Martha, who remind us of our best selves and encourage us to take steps to feel better even when we feel depleted. The tipping point tipping towards change often involves a precipitating event and some additional nudges. For Joan, the precipitating event was her granddaughter's comment. Joan felt blindsided by the comment because she was virtually blind to how her shopping habit had created a critical problem.

Joan spent months feeling hurt and defensive, waiting for her daughter to notice. When Savannah didn't say much about Joan's withdrawn behavior, Joan felt even worse. It took Martha's question to nudge Joan towards getting help. Martha instinctively knew that Joan would benefit from additional nudging to contact the therapist. Martha was prepared to back off if that wasn't what Joan wanted.

After Joan re-started therapy, the counselor recommended that Joan hire an organizer-coach. Reconnecting with her therapist proved helpful. The process uncovered the role shopping played as Joan's coping strategy and her mixed feelings in the relationship with her daughter. Joan discovered that having no physical space for her daughter unconsciously avoided their communication problems. Joan hadn't learned skills for direct communication. These skills could be learned and practiced during therapy. If Joan continued to shop as a way to distract herself or to temporarily boost her mood, then the clutter would reoccur.

Over-shopping

Shopping is an American pastime. Clothing, wall hangings, greeting cards, and many other products glorify shopping as a hobby using catchy sayings like "Shop till you drop," "Queen of shopping," and "Retail therapy." Like anything, shopping isn't necessarily problematic until it becomes excessive. Shopping can be an addiction. Unlike other addictions, American culture displays jokes about over-shopping in a way that normalizes the habit, including those I mentioned above. We wouldn't expect someone to go around wearing a t-shirt that says "Queen of Cocaine" or "I Need a Little Gambling Therapy."

I love to save money as much as the next person. Growing up with little money helped me to become resourceful to finding coupons or making do with something less expensive or that I already have. I take pride in how much I can save with grocery store coupons, and I always look online to see if I can save money via a coupon code before buying items from some retailers. These behaviors lead to certain beliefs about who I believe I am. Let's look at some common identity beliefs around shopping. Check ones that apply to you.

- ❑ I know how to get a good deal.
- ❑ Only stupid people pay full price.
- ❑ I feel proud of myself when I buy something on sale.
- ❑ I know the secrets of finding the best bargains.

What would you add to this list of beliefs?

Why We Buy

Have you heard of "Spaving?" A combination of "spend" and "save," it means spending to save money. Retailers use this method to encourage consumers to buy more in order to save more. What's left out of the conversation is that you save the most by not buying at all. Retailers understand the psychology of buying behavior. Nothing in a store's design is accidental, from having a desirable item in the back of the store to the lighting, height of items, and the add-ons located by the checkout. If they can lure you to their physical or online site, they are often able to lead you to complete the purchase.

Sellers create short time deadlines to create a buying event. Black Friday, Prime day, and coupons, in general, aim to get you to that site at a specific time. Otherwise, you will miss out. When a deal expires on a certain date, it creates price uncertainty. Limited-edition or limited-time-only products emphasize the potential for regret by not making a timely purchase. This also plays into the treasure hunt aspect of shopping. Stores like Ross, Marshall's and T.J. Max sell merchandise from other retailers and are constantly getting new things in without being able to predict how much or in what sizes. Similar to resale stores, you don't know what you might find from day to day. People who shop at these stores looking for deals are bound to find them since the hunt is broadly defined as "finding treasures."

Another retail strategy is nurturing a feeling of connectedness. Shopping channels excel at this. The exchange between the attractive host and a caller feels special. The at-home viewer is by proxy included in that specialness when she buys the product. Tweens create "haul videos" where they run through what they just bought. Others watch those videos and want to experience the thrill of the haul as well. Retailers spend big bucks sending online influencers products to review or even just to handle. Did you know that touching products makes you want to buy them? YouTube channels dedicated to "unboxing," show someone opening a box she received in the mail, pull out the interior boxing, remove the product, touch it, and describe it. Some videos only show the unboxer's hands. When my son was twelve, he watched these often and commented that the quality of the box meant that what was inside was better quality.

Retailers have trained us to believe that buying in bulk is always the better deal, although this isn't necessarily true. Stockpiling a bulk buy loses its value when the item goes bad, reduces the space available for living, causes relational conflict, and means you spend money you don't have. Besides the obvious sign of having overly full spaces, stacks of unopened packages from online shopping may indicate that your buying is out of control. Perhaps your thrill comes more from purchasing an item than from using it.

When you shop, you get something out of the deal—a physical object—but did you know buying gives you something else? It changes your brain chemistry. According to neurobiologist David Sulzer, when you get into a shopping environment, your brain begins to anticipate the purchase, sending a surge of dopamine—a chemical responsible for pleasurable feelings—to your brain.

Shopping can function like other addictions such as gambling or using smartphones. The reward centers of your brain are fed, making you feel great, at least temporarily. Once you get home, shopping bags may be set aside, unemptied. From your brain's point of view, you have already achieved the goal. Looking at piles of still-full shopping bags sitting in your hallways, however, does not feel good. Stemming the flow of new belongings coming in must happen in conjunction with getting through a clutter backlog. You can alter your approach to buying by exploring why you over-shop and being informed about how businesses aim to influence you. Dr. April Lane Benson specializes in helping people with over-shopping behaviors at https://www.shopaholicnomore.com.

Let's look at a couple of experiments that Joan (and perhaps you) could try to get more information about the role of shopping in your life and emotional regulation.

Tool #1 "Should I Buy This?" Decision Tree

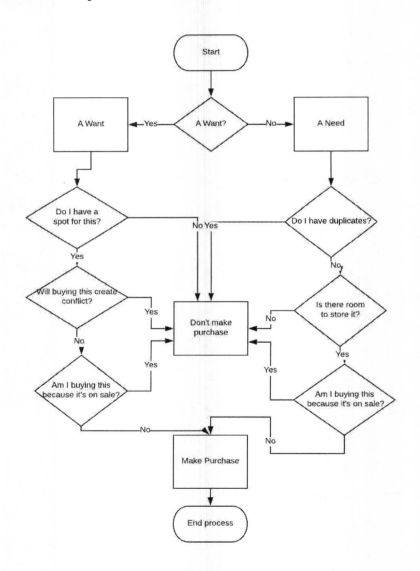

Take a photo of this decision tree on your phone and open it up next time you are shopping. Practice going through it with each item you might buy. Notice how you feel during the exercise and what you are or are not resisting. Because you are only trying this for a short time, let yourself try on different behaviors. You don't have to commit to a big change at this time, only commit to noticing your reaction when you take a new approach.

Tool #2 Create a Buying Pause

Creating a pause allows you to evaluate your buying decision outside of the stimulation of the moment. Retailers online and in-store cultivate environments to stimulate impulsive behavior. In fact, they benefit because you make impulsive decisions to buy extra from a buy-two-get-one-free sale or an add-on at the register. What might a buying pause look like? Some brick and mortar stores will hold merchandise for you for a few hours. Online, you can put items in your shopping cart and then go to a different room. If you are shopping from a paper catalog, you can tear out the page or fold the corner of the page then set the catalog aside to "marinate" until a later point.

Each of these methods may help you to step out of the emotionally activated zone and gain perspective on whether buying the item is a wise decision for your home and your pocketbook. Experiment for a set amount of time—such as one week or one month—with a different buying habit. Notice how you react. What is difficult and what is easy? Are you finding your mood to be better or worse? Has the shopping functioned as a way to avoid other feelings? How might those underlying feelings be addressed more directly? Noticing your reaction and being able to process it with someone may be valuable. Remember it's not the job of the listener to give advice; instead, the listener asks questions, remains curious, and stays quiet while the other person makes her own connections.

Joan's Habit Action Plan

What needs to be done: Take a look at her shopping habits.

What to do with it: Examine how she currently sets up her shopping plans for holidays, birthdays, and her expectation of how much to have on hand.

Where to start: Make a list of when and for whom she gives gifts within each year.

When: Between her appointments with the organizer-coach.

Who: Joan will make a list to share her experience with her organizer-coach.

Joan will:

- Create the list;
- Share it with the organizer-coach at the beginning of their next session;
- Be aware that there may be a big difference between where she is and where she wants to be as far as quantity;
- Notice aspects of this process that may be good to discuss at therapy; and
- Figure out what to do with the excess.

The Organizer-Coach will:

- Provide accountability for Joan to get the list made;
- Help Joan compare the list with the stockpile of gifts;

- Notice aspects of this process that may be good to discuss at therapy; and
- Sort the gifts into categories and help figure out where the excess will go.

Your Turn – Pause & Notice

- For what occasions do you buy gifts?
- How many gifts do you want to have on hand for last minute birthday gifts? What type of gifts is good to have on hand for this?
- How many hostess gifts or small gifts do you want to have on hand? What kinds of gifts are good for this category?
- How do you prefer to give gifts: gift bags; using wrapping paper; gift cards or money in a greeting card; something else?
- What from Joan's story resonated with you?
- What action steps will you take around gift giving and wrapping supplies?

Take a photo of your gift wrap area and gift stockpile.

Discovery Questions

- What is a turning point in your life where you could have done one thing, but instead you did another?
- What made you take that path? Do you have any regrets? How did that decision make you into who you are?

- What's something you always yearned to have but didn't get? Who would you be if you had gotten it? How have you adjusted in your life without it?

CHAPTER 5

I Now Pronounce You Full of Clutter

"When we let go of our battles and open our heart to things as they are, then we come to rest in the present moment. This is the beginning and the end of spiritual practice."
Jack Kornfield

Lisa and Richard's Story

Lisa and Richard found themselves in a not so honeymoon-ish mood five months after their wedding. When they planned to combine their two households, it sounded easy. But their experience proved otherwise. In fact, Lisa secretly wondered if she was repeating mistakes of her last marriage. With her son still in middle school, she didn't think either of them could navigate another divorce.

Tempers were short regarding the tall stacks of Lisa's boxes in the garage and the basement, and the lingering boxes still taped shut or half-unpacked in nearly every room. Kitchen drawers were crammed with duplicate utensils, and specialty cooking equipment was shoved into any available cabinet space.

Mornings meant reaching over piles of clothes and searching through baskets for something to wear. While Richard's house was bigger than Lisa's had been, his closets were smaller. Both of them need to significantly downsize wardrobes or they would have to turn the office into a walk-in closet. They attempted one Saturday of working together sorting their clothes. Their efforts ended with arguments about Lisa having too many clothes and Richard being too critical.

Richard seemed to think that his remarks would motivate Lisa to finish unpacking—as if the job were all hers. When Lisa suggested that Richard pull out his unused kitchen utensils and appliances, Richard said he would, but didn't follow through.

Lisa stayed too long in her last marriage. She knew that Richard was different and wondered if some outside help would improve their communication. Her ex didn't even consider counseling. She hoped Richard would.

On their six-month wedding anniversary dinner, Lisa summoned the courage to suggest couples counseling. Richard's reaction surprised her. He felt overwhelmed, too. They agreed to call his friend's marriage therapist the following Monday.

Perhaps by filling out one of these charts individually, then one as a couple, Lisa and Richard will notice some of their unspoken and spoken perspectives and how things have or have not been communicated. We'll just look at Lisa's.

Lisa's Tipping Point

PAIN OF REMAINING THE SAME	PAIN OF CHANGING	BENEFITS OF CHANGING
Continued arguments	Arguments about who gets to keep what	Better communication, with help from the counselor
Chaotic mornings	The expense of hiring help	Getting ready in the morning will be easier
Feeling unsettled	Time to go through it	Ease with finding and

		putting away clothes
Worry that the relationship will shift to divorce	What if she gets divorced again and she needs her kitchen stuff?	Cooking and cleaning up will be something they can do together
Not a good environment for her son		Lisa's son can help with chores, and his stress levels will be less
Spending money on take-out food and restaurants		Not living among boxes and unfinished tasks
		Being "all in" with the relationship where they are both committed

Visualize Success

- Success would look like a kitchen which functions, where items fit into the cabinets that are available and when there are duplicates, the couple decides which one is in the best condition.
- Success would mean everyone can find the clothes they like to wear.
- Success would feel like mornings that run more smoothly.

Project Action Plan Pre-Work

In a marriage therapy meeting before the kitchen organizing session, Lisa and Richard came up with **ground rules**, which they posted in their kitchen:

- Their common goal was to have a functioning kitchen where cabinets and drawers were not crowded, and duplicates were eliminated wherever possible.

- In general, they would choose the duplicate in better condition.

- They would try to balance how much each of them was giving or keeping.

- Each person got three "free passes" for individual items without having to justify the choice.

- If they both wanted to keep their version of the same thing, they would each rate the duplicate with a: 1-highly important, 2-somewhat important, or 3-important on a post-it note, then set this item aside until later. They would revisit each ranked category at the end to see if they could make a decision. If a decision still couldn't be made, the items would be brought to their next therapy session.

- They could decide on items playfully by rolling a dice or playing rock, paper, scissors.

- They could get rid of both duplicates and buy a new one.

- Anyone could ask for a five-minute break if he or she needed it.

Lisa and Richard's Project Action Plan

Goal: To set up a functioning kitchen where cabinets and drawers are not crowded, and duplicates are eliminated wherever possible.

What needs to be done: Combine the items from Lisa's and Richard's kitchens.

What to do with it: Keep the duplicate in better condition, donate the rest, and organize the kitchen with what is kept.

Where to start: Kitchen related boxes from the garage and basement will be brought to the kitchen/dining area, where temporary tables are set up. Like items are pulled from the cabinets and boxes and set up on the tables to be sorted first. Decisions will not be made until *after* the items are sorted in categories. At that point, Lisa and Richard will go through by category to decide what to keep and what to donate.

When: Saturday at 9 a.m.

Who: Richard, Lisa, and a team of two professional organizers.

Lisa and Richard will:

- Keep focused on the initial stage of gathering kitchen boxes and identifying like items during the sorting process, but not making decisions yet;

- Notice if they were feeling overwhelmed by seeing so much stuff out all at once and wanted to take a break rather than say unkind words;

- Use the "I feel" technique they learned in therapy: "I feel worried that if we don't get rid of more, we won't reach our goal;"

- Reread the ground rules for ideas on how to negotiate decision-making, and set aside items that need deeper negotiation;
- Practice the "I appreciate" technique they learned in therapy: "I appreciate that you and I are working on this together;" and
- Remember that was okay to have fun during the process of creating their home together.

The Organizers will:
- Help locate unpacked boxes of kitchen stuff and bring them to the kitchen/dining area;
- Provide temporary sorting tables and set them up in the kitchen/dining area;
- Gather like items together on the tables: dishes, mixing supplies, bakeware, kitchen appliances, serving dishes, barware, etc. One organizer will assist Richard to pull these items from the kitchen, while the other organizer will assist Lisa to pull these items from the boxes;
- Remind Lisa and Richard to not make decisions during the sorting process so that the overall process will go more quickly and smoothly;
- Help Lisa and Richard decide on each category, using the ground rules;
- Affirm Lisa and Richard working together well;
- Box up donations or trash;
- Work with Lisa and Richard to create a plan for how to maximize the kitchen space as items get put away; and
- Notice everyone's energy levels and the time and initiating breaks when needed.

When Zombies Attack

Stuff and Emotional Baggage

The process of Lisa and Richard combining homes might have been doomed without the marriage therapist—whom they both like. Lisa and Richard each had a house full of stuff and plenty of emotional baggage. While the physical stuff was visible, the invisible emotional baggage took the form of mini-battles. What might have appeared to be an argument about a wet towel left on the bathroom floor was really about bigger issues: *Is my loved one listening to me? How important are my needs to him or her? Is he or she overreacting*?

Leaving one dysfunctional relationship doesn't change the fact that you bring yourself to the next one. That's only a problem if you haven't done the necessary work to heal. No divorce is the fault of one person, no matter how awful that person's behavior or betrayal was. Even the spouse who was wronged played a role and can gain skills to have healthier relationships in the future. Dr. Harville Hendrix and Dr. Helen LaKelly Hunt developed Imago Relationship Therapy based on the idea that adult relationships often connect to early childhood experiences. For example, if you were neglected as a child, you will be hyper-alert to not receiving attention from your partner. By unconsciously drawing to you someone who repeats the behavior patterns of your parent, you have the opportunity as an adult to heal this unhealed part of yourself. You will continue to draw these people into your life until you learn the necessary lessons and move towards wholeness.

Just because you have the opportunity to become more whole, doesn't mean you will do the work. Some people may not be able to acknowledge their role in the dysfunction because they think admitting feelings makes them look weak. Maybe they lack the skills to work through their feelings. These people are unlikely to consider therapy as an option. Lisa's first husband fell into this category, and eventually, Lisa realized the only way for her to get unstuck was divorce. When one person in a relationship refuses to attend therapy, the other person can pursue individual therapy. Even if you suspect the relationship will not survive, going to therapy to heal yourself is an investment in your own future well-being.

To get the most from therapy, find a therapist with whom you feel fully supported. If you don't feel supported and heard, release that person from your team and continue your quest to find a good match until you find one. I give you permission to fire your therapist, doctor, housecleaner, organizer, or any service person that does not support you in the ways you want them to. Life is too short to undermine yourself because you are afraid to "hurt someone's feelings" by dismissing them. Building your support team is one of the best ways to acknowledge that you value yourself.

Here's the deal with therapy: it's not necessary to have the other person there to make changes in you. You may think everything would be magically better if the other person stopped dropping his wet towel on the bathroom floor—and maybe it would be somewhat better—but his behavior change will not fix your ability to clearly ask for what you want. If you have a habit of expecting your spouse to read your mind and then feel disappointed when he cannot consider getting assistance with the issues within your power.

The Trouble with Mindreading

I used to have a problem with mindreading, meaning I thought the problem was my husband couldn't read my mind. How I wished I would get flowers spontaneously delivered to me! Wasn't giving flowers how loving husbands made their wives feel special? Didn't my husband watch Hallmark Channel movies? (Okay, he didn't.) I couldn't tell him directly I wanted flowers because I believed it wouldn't count; it meant he was only giving me flowers because I told him to and not because he wanted to. I felt bitterly disappointed that he didn't just know what he "should" be doing.

Then I read a magazine article explaining how I could drop a hint of wanting flowers by leaving out an empty vase. I thought that was too subtle, so instead, I placed the empty vase in a very odd place: my husband's pillow on our bed. I waited several days, sure that at any time, the flowers would arrive. Days turned into two weeks and still nothing.

Finally, I confronted him, "Did you see that empty vase on your pillow?"

He nodded and replied, "Yeah, I couldn't figure out why it was there, so I just moved it."

At that moment I realized that my mindreading approach was not working. I had set-up an unwinnable situation for him, which continued to deliver disappointment to me. I explained my feelings to him, and he was surprised. Certainly, he wanted me to feel special, and he didn't know that flowers were such a big deal to me. He vowed to do better with giving flowers, and I vowed to express my needs more explicitly.

Working Together

Lisa and Richard combining their belongings presents them with the opportunity to clarify what each of them wants. The dilemma isn't whose mixing bowls will work the best; it's about whether Richard will listen to Lisa explain how the bowls were a gift from her mother for Lisa's first apartment. Perhaps this means that Lisa's bowls carry more weight in the decision-making process. The dilemma involves whether Lisa will acknowledge how uncomfortable Richard feels by having overly full cabinets and cluttered counters. Battles are only battles when the couple sees each other as adversaries. When they see each other as part of a team, those decisions become compromises, where the give and take dynamic affirms each other's needs.

Lisa and Richard's Habit Action Plan

What needs to be done: Practice communication using their ground rules list and new skills in a small space.

What to do with it: Combine personal care items.

Where to start: Master Bathroom.

When: Saturday morning at 10 a.m.

Who: Lisa and Richard.

Richard will:

- Remove his things from the bathroom cabinets, place them in a box and bring them to the master bed, which will be his sorting space;
- Keep personal care items that he uses and that are still good;

- Toss personal care items that are expired, mostly used up, or that he doesn't use;

- Wipe out the cabinet drawers and other storage areas;

- Negotiate the division of space with Lisa, once each knows how much they are keeping; and

- Believe Lisa when she says she needs more stuff than him.

Lisa will:

- Gather all of her personal care items on her side of the bed and begin sorting;

- Keep what she uses and is still good;

- Toss personal care items that are expired, mostly used up, or that she doesn't use;

- Acknowledge that Richard wants a cleared off counter and ask for the extra space she needs;

- Create "getting ready kits" such as a "hair styling kit" and a "makeup kit" that can easily be pulled out and put away; and

- Consider alternate spaces for storing her back-up toiletries.

Your Turn: Pause & Notice

- What are some areas where you and another person need to negotiate stuff and emotional baggage?

- If you are combining households due to remarriage or looking to downsize from your joint home of many years, how will you split the decision areas?

- What decision ground rules would you adopt or add?

- What from Lisa and Richard's story resonated with you?

- Could you and your partner benefit from therapy? You by yourself? What would cause you to move forward to get that support?

Take a photo of one area where you and a loved one need to work together to reduce or combine.

Discovery Questions

- Think about someone you admire. What qualities does he or she have? How does he or she show those qualities?

- When have you shown those qualities?

SECTION 2:

Realign Vocation

CHAPTER 6

Filling the Days of Our Lives

"We cannot live in the afternoon of life according to the program of life's morning."
Carl Jung

The Daily Grind

Remember being in high school and having people ask you what you wanted to do when you grew up? Maybe you knew at a young age what job you wanted, maybe your parents or society dictated what your path, or maybe you stumbled upon work that led to your career. Whatever way you got there, you've spent a large part of your life engaged in work—however meaningful, tedious, or neutral that experience has been.

The focus of this section is career or vocation. The word vocation stems from the Latin word *vocare*, meaning "to call." In my opinion, the best-case career scenario calls upon someone's unique combination of temperament, talents, and life experience. It's not always possible for a calling to come via career, though. Sometimes a person's vocation is fulfilled through volunteering or another role. Finding and pursuing your life calling can bring the greatest levels of life satisfaction. Let's examine the aspects that have been most satisfying in your life and see how those can be modified as you transition in your career.

Retirement is one example of a career transition, but certainly not the only one. Americans have more job fluidity now than they did fifty years ago when people worked for the same boss their whole lives. According to the Bureau of Labor Statistics, people born from 1957 to 1964 held an average of eleven point seven jobs between ages eighteen and forty-eight. Millennials are more likely to hold more jobs over their lifetimes. Changing jobs is another example of a career transition. A new position requires you to build on existing skills or develop new ones. A stay-at-home mother doesn't stop being a mom when she rejoins the workforce, but that change does mark a career transition—one that can feel like a relief or be quite daunting, depending upon how long she was an at-home mom. When we change jobs, we expect there to be an adjustment period, and the same is true for when we retire.

In Chapter 1, we looked at examples of expected and unexpected transitions, and ones that you may expect, but that kind of sneak up on you. Remember the example of the mom who intentionally prepared her kid to go to college, but haphazardly prepared herself for her own changes. I proposed shifting to more intentional transitions by planning in three areas: what skills are necessary, what stuff will you want, and who can help you transition. We will apply those three to career transitions.

Normative and Non-Normative Transitions

Transitions—whether personal or in your career—may follow a normative pattern, which means there are a general order and timing of life events in society. A normative pattern might include life events in this order: going to school, beginning your career, getting married, buying a home, and having children. Most people expect transitions to follow a normative pattern. Society tends to reward people for following the patterns by supporting transitions that follow the norm. Society tends to be unsupportive towards people who don't follow norms. How many times can unmarried thirty-somethings be asked when they will marry before they start avoiding the questioners?

Anticipated career transitions that follow a normative pattern can be somewhat easier to navigate than anticipated transitions that occur outside expected norms. Officemates throw a retirement party for someone moving to Florida to play golf, but may not have a party for someone who retires from his job to provide full-time care for his wife. It's not that office mates don't support the person who becomes a caregiver as much as the first example fills the normative pattern. Societal support and individual support systems may not respond as readily depending upon whether the transition fits norms or doesn't. And without support, a transition can feel like a crisis.

Anticipated and Unanticipated Career Transitions

Unanticipated transitions may also be difficult to navigate due to the abrupt shift in expectations. Going through a serious illness, having a loved one die, experiencing a traumatic event like a natural disaster or being the victim of a crime are all examples of unanticipated and unwelcome transitions. Unanticipated transitions can be positive as well—such as winning the lottery. Such a change would bring both happiness and difficulties as you adjust. Losing your job is an example of an unanticipated career transition. These types of transitions—whether welcome or unwelcome—provide an even greater catalyst for taking action that anticipated transitions. The expected need to downsize your house sparks a less immediate reaction than the unexpected event of your house burning down. If you get fired, you have to find another job quickly. Getting a divorce may mean you need a higher-paying career. The timing of transitions which you anticipate is more often within your control, whereas your locus of control with unanticipated transitions lies more within your reaction to them.

What does this mean for career transitions? Let's bring in the skills, stuff, and help trio to compare how you can be intentional with both anticipated and unanticipated career changes.

Anticipated career transition of retirement

What **skills** are necessary?

- ✓ Finding a new routine
- ✓ Maintaining social connections
- ✓ Financial management
- ✓ Prioritizing interests and hobbies
- ✓ Getting used to being with your spouse all the time
- ✓ Renegotiating household tasks

What **stuff** will you want?

- ✓ Supplies for interests and hobbies
- ✓ Fewer things so you can have more experiences

Who can **help** you transition?

- ✓ Friends, colleagues, online groups, continuing education providers

Unanticipated career transition of getting laid off

What **skills** are necessary?

- ✓ A plan for sharpening or increasing knowledge
- ✓ Networking
- ✓ Leaning new platforms for finding jobs
- ✓ Financial management to get by

✓ Creating a new resume

What **stuff** will you want?

✓ Interview clothes

✓ Access to the internet

✓ Access to transportation

Who can **help** you transition?

✓ Friends, job search companies, local career training office, community college, online learning resource

The primary difference between the two career transitions above is the sense of urgency needed with the second example. That urgency drives action, unless you are in a state of shock and denial that the unanticipated happened. This first hurdle of acknowledging that the thing happened is something we'll explore with William Bridge's Model of Transition below. With an anticipated career transition like retirement, there's little need to accept that it happened. Having the control of initiating a change is generally a good thing. One exception to this is if you want to shift your career focus. Without an outside push to change jobs, you may be tempted to put off identifying the skills, stuff, and help required to initiate a job change. Let me say it plainly, if you want to shift your career, find ways to light a fire under yourself.

Even with an anticipated career change, unanticipated elements can create a feeling of crisis. About one-third of retirees enter retirement abruptly and not at the time of their choosing. Lacking control over retirement complicates having a smooth transition and may trigger some of the negative feelings experienced at the onset of an unanticipated transition.

What Aids Transitions

What can help with an abrupt change in career is to create structure in your day, not just with activities that keep you busy, but ones that increase a positive sense of purpose. Another helpful response if you feel overwhelmed is to get outside of yourself to help others. Volunteering doesn't have to involve anything dramatic. The secret to feeling better immediately is to do an act of kindness for someone else. Pay for the meal of the person behind you in the drive-thru, call or email someone and tell them how much they mean to you, or smile warmly at the store employee who scans your purchase. All of these acts will improve your well-being and assist you to get through a life transition.

Gradual retirement may be the best option, as there's a slow progression to divest responsibilities. People using this approach often fare better because they feel more in control. In addition, how you spend your time during the day is not such a stark change because you still interact with co-workers or clients, just not as much. Retiring gradually can look like finishing at your old workplace, but taking on new paid or volunteer consulting that utilizes your expertise and continues your sense of relevance.

Although you cannot always control all the details of a career change like retirement, you can design it—with intention—to fit your needs. The age at which people retire is changing. Ten thousand Baby Boomers retire every day. According to a 2017 Gallup poll, "nearly 40% of Americans now believe they will retire after age sixty-five—a stark departure from their beliefs in the 1990s." Another change Boomers have introduced is the concept of "unretirement." To unretire means to retire and then return to the workforce either in their previous career or a completely different one. Some popular jobs for people who unretire include driver, retail worker, tutor, tour guide, and culinary worker. Find out what other career you might want to have by taking the quiz at www.unretireyourself.com/resources/quiz/.

Bridge's Transition Model

Adjusting to life transitions happens over time. Although each person experiences the process uniquely, it's helpful to look at how people generally engage in the stages of transition. William Bridge's model of transition, illustrated below, begins with a precipitating event, which is often unanticipated. Think of it as though you have been dropped into a new world like *Alice in Wonderland* where familiar rules do not apply. This feels unsettling and disorienting. Unlike Alice, adults who enter this process have to acknowledge that things have changed.

The first stage marks the end of life as it was. To pick up on a previous example, you've been laid off. You are flooded with emotions, and ninety-nine percent of them are negative. Perhaps you feel side-swiped and did not see it coming. Maybe you have a sense of injustice that you were laid off instead of someone else who produces less. You don't like what's happening, and you don't want to accept it. Of the many feelings you can see in the illustration, fear of the unknown is a powerfully paralyzing one.

With your emotions heightened, you don't have a clear idea of how to address the situation. Your desire to hold on to the past may be a bit out of proportion. It's like you are in the ocean but cannot touch the bottom. After trying to tread water for a while, you get tired and realize that resisting the situation isn't getting you anywhere but tired. This glimmer of wanting relief will carry you forward into the next stage. Naming the emotions that also helps.

Stage two, the neutral zone, means you are temporarily in-between the old and new experiences, and neither place feels quite right. Eventually, you realize you must let go of the old assumptions about how things should go and open up to new ways of understanding the transition. Remember that word liminal from Chapter 1? This stage reflects that. Uncertainty and anxiety still reign, but are combined with impatience to have a reprieve and frustration that you seem to be getting nowhere.

Take heart, though. Enlist the support of others and look for quick wins to help you see that a new reality is possible. The laid-off worker can take a friend's advice to submit an application. He can search for resources and discover a free career seminar at the city's Health and Human Services Department. He may still be overwhelmed, but is not as hopeless. Having a mindset of curiosity and inquiry will serve you well to reach the final stage.

Stage three marks a new beginning, bringing relief and a sense of accomplishment. All transitions alter routines, roles, and relationships. In this stage, you are learning new skills, trying out new routines, renegotiating what relationships will look like since your life changed. The creativity and innovation that can occur in this stage reenergize you after the discouragement of stage one and the low productivity of stage two. It may seem like you still have a lot to learn to get to a new sense of normal, and that may be tiring. As you accept the reality of what happened and initiate actions to respond, you will find your way, especially with support and encouragement.

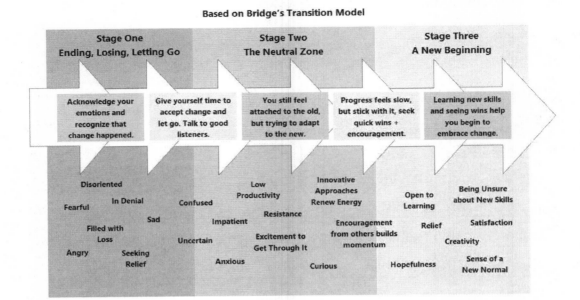

Based on Bridge's Transition Model

Taking Stock of Your Vocation

Whether you've already retired, are going to retire soon, or are looking to shift your career, it's valuable to take stock of where your career stands now.

- What is your current job situation?
- How did you expect your career to be at this life stage?
- Where do you see yourself in Bridge's transition model and what emotions are you experiencing?
- What skills could help you navigate career change?
- What items related to previous jobs are no longer necessary?
- Who are your allies in the process of career transition?

How Do You Measure Career Success?

We have defined what success looks and feels like in the preceding chapters. Now we'll turn to what success means for your career, and by extension, your life. In your opinion, what makes someone successful? External measurements include having a high income, owning property, being seen as a community leader, producing something tangible that others can enjoy, reaching benchmarks such as 50 years of marriage or 100 years old, and many other outwardly visible markers. Internal measurements are harder for others to quantify, but I'd venture to say that these are the more satisfying success yardsticks. Many people equate one's legacy to outward signs of success. In Chapter 11, we'll dig deeper into the concept of defining your legacy. Here, we will gather information about your external success markers, particularly related to vocation.

- What are some of your career achievements so far?
- What other externally measured successes would you like to have (financial, career, civic, or societal)?
- What groups would you like to make a difference in? Who do you feel called to serve?

Finding Life Satisfaction via Activities

Pursuing your passions and hobbies brings joy at every life stage, and is especially important after career change like retirement. Before retirement, you may have longed for some time with no outside commitments or demands, anticipating how many long-delayed projects you could accomplish.

After the initial thrill of retirement passes, you may find yourself with lots of unclaimed days which pass without you doing much of anything. If your aim was doing more of nothing, then congratulations, you've succeeded.

If, however, you want to pursue certain hobbies or tick off important to-dos on your list, then you need to be more specific about how you'll spend your time. Fuzzy goals create fuzzy results. And too many fuzzy days are not good for your brain. Being physically and mentally active keeps you sharp, making you feel better. Now is the time to have fun, try new things, and finish those projects. In Chapter 1, I talked about the importance of finding things to be excited about. So, let's do that.

- What's on your bucket list for the next year? Come up with at least 20 things, small or big.
- What activities did you enjoy as a child?
- What hobbies aren't enjoyable anymore?
- What would you try if you knew you couldn't fail?

Finding Life Satisfaction via Activities and Social Connection

Combining your interests and engaging with others stimulates your brain while reducing your loneliness. An unfortunate part of getting older is having friends and loved ones die or move away. Combine that with the loss of social interaction post-retirement, and it's easy to see how someone could feel depressed and isolated. Friendships are essential for many reasons. Friends support you through difficulty and help you feel accepted instead of judged and dismissed. Having someone to share private things with alleviates the sense that you are alone in this world. At the very least you have a partner in fun and for activities, and you have a link to the outside world.

You can have different levels of friendships—ones you occasionally meet for lunch, ones who share common interests, ones with whom you share secrets—but some kind of social connection is essential. When you feel low on friends because of circumstances beyond your control, find ways to continue to have social interaction even when the quality doesn't equal what you previously had. Your life satisfaction and longevity depend upon it.

Finding new friends may be less challenging than you think. Friendships begun later in life are often based on interests and values. Search the internet for: groups + [your interest] + [your city]. You will find results from public and private organizations in your area—like a library, museum, arboretum, community college, hobby store, etc.—that sponsor free or low fee activities. In-person groups are best, but online groups will work, too. Here are just a few ideas to get you started:

- **Interest-based groups**: theater, arts, traveling, nature walks, gardening, book clubs, model train clubs, genealogists, writers, or sewing groups.
- **Values-based groups**: political party, religious group, or social issue group.
- Activities that are slightly **out of your comfort zone**: Escape room, Improv classes, singing lessons, cooking classes, paint night, or language club.

Find groups online that pair you with someone who needs your skills. These are just a few options:

- Experience Corps connects adults over age fifty-five with kids who need help to improve their reading skills. https://www.aarp.org/experience-corps/
- Senior Corps pairs older adults who can serve as foster grandparents and senior companions. https://www.nationalservice.gov/programs/senior-corps
- Big Brothers, Big Sisters matches adults with children who need mentors. https://www.bbbs.org/

Be the Hero of Your Own Social Life

- Find new friends by striking up conversations at restaurants, the movies, events, and even in line at the grocery store!
- If you know other people in the same situation as you, try an experiment where you set a standing date to get together. For example, every Wednesday morning at 9 a.m. whoever can meet goes to Panera or McDonald's or wherever your favorite hangout spot might be.

The Greatest Measure of Success: Friends

In the 1946 movie, *It's a Wonderful Life*, George Bailey owned a Savings and Loan that was only solvent because of George's generosity to his customers. When his forgetful uncle misplaced a bank deposit of $8,000 (equivalent to $112,000 today), George faced not only the end of his business but the possibility of going to jail. Unable to secure a loan using his life insurance policy as collateral, George realized he was worth more dead than alive. In his desperation, he believed everyone would be better off if he ended his life by jumping off a bridge. At this critical moment, George's guardian angel appeared.

While I find the story of George compelling, I'm even more fascinated by the character Clarence Oddfellow, a second-class angel sent down from heaven to help George see the value of his life. If Clarence is successful, he will earn his wings and become a first-class angel. The head angels described Clarence as having the "intelligence of a rabbit" and "the faith of a child." His simplicity held its own powerful wisdom. Clarence knew who he was so completely that he made no attempts to hide from strangers (the bridge guard, Nick the bartender) that he was a 292-year-old angel. He was who he was without trying to prove anything to anyone. What better person to remind George of his own values and character? Clarence didn't wait until George was on the rail to try to talk him out of it; instead, Clarence jumped in, knowing that George was the kind of person who would jump in to save Clarence. In this way, George was saved from his uncharacteristic intentions to harm himself because his true self stepped in to save Clarence.

Clarence's wisdom as a guardian angel was not to fix things for George or to lecture about why he shouldn't kill himself. Instead, he granted George's wish of seeing what life would have been like if George had never been born. Clarence accompanied George through his dark night of the soul as he began to see for himself the value of his life. Our hero George saw how every battle he fought and won throughout his life affected not just him and the people he knew he had helped, but the whole town. The town would have been prey to greedy Mr. Potter. When George saved his nine-year-old brother from drowning, it created a ripple effect far beyond his town when his brother later saved a ship full of soldiers. Clarence only needed to stand in the background while George experienced the different stages of understanding until he finally understood. George ran back to the bridge, searching for Clarence because he wanted his life back—even if that meant he would go to jail and lose his material possessions.

There, at the bridge, George gained not only his life, but he also gained a new perspective. George, ready to accept any reality that awaited him, rushed back to his house to find his family. While he was working through his dark night of the soul, his wife and uncle contacted all of the people who George had helped. They piled into George's house with money to replace the lost bank deposit. More than saving him from losing his business and going to jail, George's friends reinforced how rich George was in kindness, love, and friendship. What George (and viewers) so viscerally experience in this beautiful final scene was confirmed by the inscription in Clarence's book, which suddenly appeared on top of the money pile. Now a first-class angel, Clarence wrote, "Remember, no man is a failure who has friends."

Clarence could not have told George this sentence at the beginning of the movie and had the same effect. It would have merely been unwanted advice— a platitude given by someone who didn't know anything. We've all been in a low spot where someone has tried to offer their advice on how to fix it. Not very helpful, is it? The most valuable transformation occurs when someone experiences it himself. This is not a solitary pursuit. George could not have gotten there himself. That's why I'm so frustrated by the concept of self-help. When you are desperate and in crisis, your brain is not thinking of who you really are. Your perspective is skewed. We all need guardian angels and friends to protect us—sometimes from ourselves—by reminding us of our true character. Clarence's most impactful deed was to jump into the river, prompting George to be his true self: a strong, generous person, not afraid to act in service of others.

Your guardian angel functions as a witness to your journey, a supporter, and a reminder that you are not alone. If you haven't yet found a companion for this process, I invite you to continue your search. It will help you to gain perspective as you examine your transitions in your career and life.

Discovery Questions

- What's a childhood dream you never accomplished? How would things be different if you had done that?

- Tell me about something you accomplished by age 18. Were you in a sport, did you save up money for a car, win an award?

- Tell me about a success you had during your career? What made this possible?

CHAPTER 7

So Many Books, So Little Time

"When faced with any difficulty of life, resolve it by following these four steps: face it, accept it, deal with it, and then let it go."
Sheng-yen

Gwen's Story

Gwen loved to read, and she loves to be surrounded by books. As a child she devoured books, often tenting up her bedcovers to hide her flashlight-illuminated book to read through the night.

It came as no surprise to anyone when Gwen enjoyed a long and successful career as an elementary school reading specialist and librarian. She attempted retirement three times, each time getting pulled into part-time subbing, then replacing a full-time teacher, then maternity leave subbing, and heading up the school library remodel committee.

She finally really and truly retired after a breast cancer scare. Doctors caught the cancer early, so she was in official remission after surgery. The stuff that had been such a comfort to her in the past now felt like an itchy sweater she wanted to take off. The treatment spurred Gwen to make a retirement bucket list that included traveling, reading, spending time with her daughter, son-in-law, and grandkids, and finally getting organized.

Gwen systematically purged her junk drawers and closets, old camping gear, sports equipment, kitchen items, decorations, and some furniture. Her books, though, were a completely different story.

"I'm a book hoarder," she joked to her friends, "which means I'm the smartest messy person you know." Although she laughed, she couldn't shake that uneasy feeling of wanting to be free.

All that stood in the way of selling her house to go live near her daughter were the books and her storage room boxes, which included teaching materials, textbooks, notes from students, classroom decorations, and craft items for kids. The stuff in her storage room had come in handy the first three times she tried to retire. She didn't think she would return to teaching again, but could she be sure?

Gwen couldn't imagine moving all 2,000 books and her teacher things, and she couldn't imagine getting rid of them either. Spring arrived, and so had Gwen's best opportunity to put her house on the market. As each week passed, she berated herself for not sorting the books. She seemed to be spending extra time outside of the house, being busy, and wasn't making any progress on her goal to move.

Pause & Notice

- What problems does Gwen see?
- What is making Gwen stuck?
- How did keeping books and teacher materials help Gwen in the past?
- What is Gwen giving up by letting go of some of the books and teaching materials?
- What is she gaining?
- What advice would you give Gwen?

Gwen's Tipping Point

PAIN OF REMAINING THE SAME	PAIN OF CHANGING	BENEFITS OF CHANGING
Having to store 2000 books so she can sell her house	Having to let go of books, which feels uncomfortable	Being able to sell her house easier and sooner
Having to move 2000 books and the boxes of teaching materials means more time/money	Taking the small chance of having to rebuy books or recreate teaching materials	Spending less to move
Having a crowded house at her new place or spending money on a storage unit		Knowing that her possessions will fit into her new smaller home
Knowing she has delayed decisions she will eventually have to make		Feeling free of having so much stuff
		Cherishing the very best memories from her career when they are gathered in a manageable way

Visualize Success

- Success would look like reducing her book collection by two-thirds so that it fit into ten to fifteen book-sized moving boxes. Success would mean being able to get her house on the market and move forward with her plan.

- Gwen would feel a huge sense of accomplishment after shedding the "clutter coat" and starting a new chapter of her life. Success would be the relief she felt when her belongings comfortably fit into her new home.

Gwen's Project Action Plan – Part 1: Books

Goal: Get her house on the market in two weeks.

What needs to be done: Decrease her book collection.

What to do with it: Find places to donate books and some of the teaching materials and keep only what fits in ten to fifteen book-sized moving boxes.

Where to start: Gwen identifies her paperback mystery and romance collection as the easiest place to start.

When: Monday and Wednesday from 12-4 p.m.

Who: Gwen looked online and asked around with her friends to find a local professional organizer. After calling a few, she made the appointment with the one with whom she felt most comfortable. To prepare, Gwen gathered empty boxes and some sturdy bags to hold books. She moved the stacks of paperbacks into her study.

Gwen will:

- Identify where she might donate books;

- Make a goal of how much to keep and discard;

- Quickly identify her favorite books/authors to keep;

- Let go of books she doesn't want to re-read or authors she doesn't like so much; and

- Talk through ways she gets stuck and notice when she is successful.

The Organizer will:

- Help Gwen set up categories of donating to the library book sale, sell to the used book store, and keep;

- Encourage Gwen to set a goal for how much she will keep and discard;

- Presort the books by author so Gwen can see where she might have duplicates or be able to identify her favorite author's books;

- Notice when Gwen is getting stuck and when she is having success.

- Get books into the right piles after Gwen has decided; and

- Take books to donate or to the bookseller if Gwen wishes.

The Result

Letting go of her paperbacks was easier than Gwen expected. She and the organizer got through all the paperback mysteries and romances in the whole house. They gathered books in other categories from upstairs and brought them to the main floor bookcases to work through in their follow-up session.

The books for resale were brought to a spot near the door until the rest of the books were sorted. The donate bags were placed in Gwen's car. Gwen was quite proud to have discarded two-thirds of her paperbacks and filled only thirteen book-sized moving boxes.

Gwen felt both elated and decisioned-out. After taking a break, she and the organizer pre-sorted the teaching materials boxes, separating the craft materials from the textbooks and general teaching files. These would be tackled after finishing with her books.

In working with the organizer, Gwen realized that she felt most stuck making decisions about books she had not yet read. They devised a rule that for each one she kept, she would take two to a book reseller. Key to her success was knowing how easily and inexpensively she could buy more paperbacks. She also felt really good about donating books to a nearby senior center.

After experiencing the relief of having supportive help, Gwen realized how many months she had wasted trying to sort through her books and materials alone. While it was exhausting to work so intensely, she knew that hiring someone was the only way she would have gotten the project done. The organizer boosted Gwen's confidence in the process, encouraging her to think through the "what if's."

Gwen's Project Action Plan – Part 2: Teaching Materials

What needs to be done: Not keep every paper related to her career.

What to do with it: Get her teacher materials from ten boxes down to one box of teaching related papers and one box of craft materials.

Where to start: At the last appointment they pre-sorted the teaching materials boxes in the basement, separating the craft materials from the textbooks and general teaching files.

1) They would start with the craft materials, and keep only what she believes she would use with her grandkids, aged fourteen, twelve, and ten. The rest would go to the school where she taught.

2) Next, they would tackle the papers and keep only things that:

   - Represented projects she was proudest of doing; and

   - Thank you notes and messages that reminded her of those students whom she most impacted.

3) Any textbooks and worksheets would be recycled because the material was out-of-date. Despite her reluctance to acknowledge the materials are obsolete, Gwen authorized the organizer to automatically recycle textbooks and files of worksheet duplicates.

When: Friday from 12-4 p.m.

Who: Gwen and the professional organizer who helped her with books.

Gwen will:

- Be realistic about the kinds of projects her grandkids will do as ten-to-fourteen-year-olds, remembering that she can always buy new craft materials after she moves;

- Evaluate notes and drawings from students, choosing the ones that mean the most and represent her work she as a teacher and librarian;

- Resist the temptation to think of uses for the outdated textbooks and worksheets and allow the organizer to recycle them;

- Visualize the teachers at her old school feeling happy to receive her donation of learning games and tools;

- Chose a plan for the memory papers she is keeping: which is to buy a decorative paperboard box from the craft store to hold her teaching memories. She will tuck the pretty box under an end table at her new home to look from time to time;

- Deliver the donation to her former school on Monday; and

- Celebrate the fact that she has downsized many boxes down to one small box of craft supplies and one small box of the most meaningful reminders of her career.

The Organizer will:

- Notice when Gwen's decisions are flowing and when she is second-guessing herself;

- Search the boxes for papers that Gwen might consider for her teaching memory file and hand them to her to evaluate;

- Recycle textbooks and duplicate worksheets;

- Help Gwen take photos of items she doesn't want to keep but wants to remember;

- Remind Gwen of how excited teachers at her old school will be to receive some of the hands-on learning games and tools Gwen has accumulated;

- Take out the recycling and trash at the end;

- Help place the donations in Gwen's trunk for delivery to the school; and

- Discuss with Gwen some options for displaying or storing the memory papers she is keeping.

When Zombies Attack

Books as Friends

Avid readers understand the powerful presence that books can have. Books provide a mirror of who you yearn to be, help you understand who you are, take you on great adventures, and comfort you like an old friend. Not all friends are equal, however. Sometimes you make a lifelong friend. Other times you have friends who are in your life for a short period. Still other times, you are stuck in a group of people by circumstance, and you may or may not enjoy being with them.

In her book, *Conquering Chronic Disorganization*, organizing expert Judith Kolberg suggests using an approach called "Friends, Acquaintances, and Strangers." I've found this technique to be particularly useful for clients who feel attached to certain belongings, such as collections. First, identify your "best friends" in the collection. Keep them close to you. Your reaction to the best friend books will be an instant happy feeling. Next, identify the "strangers." In this scenario, it would be books that you have no interest in reading and to which your immediate reaction is to say good-bye. What's left are the "acquaintances," which evoke ambivalence. You don't have strong feelings to keep or to get rid of these books. Most likely, the words, "I should" come up, as in, "Aunt Jane gave this coffee table book to me so I should probably keep it." Or, "I paid so much for this textbook twenty years ago that I should keep it." To which I say, WHY? If the "acquaintance" has served you but is no longer serving you, the best thing you can do is release it so that it can be a blessing for someone else.

Some say that you should only keep books you plan to read or re-read. A minimalist might say not to own any physical books. To me, how many you keep is a personal decision. We all want homes that feel comfortable to us. Defining comfort varies by person. If you feel that books are your friends, that's fine! Get rid of all of the books that aren't your best friends, and then use the remaining books as part of your décor plan. Nineteenth-century artist and designer William Morris said, "Have nothing in your house that you do not know to be useful, or believe to be beautiful."

With books, as with many collections, it seems at first glance that all are of equal importance. The truth is that they are not equally as valuable to you, just like all the people you know are not equally your friends.

Attitude of Gratitude

Japanese life organizer Marie Kondo, in her book *The Life-Changing Magic of Tidying Up*, has a wonderful technique for letting go that involves thanking the object for the role it played in your life. Let's look at how this plays out with books, starting with ones that played an important part in your life but have reached the end of their life cycle. Your very expensive textbook from twenty years ago is out of date and is not of use to donate.

"It's sacrilege to just throw it away!" you say. "How can I possibly tear out the inner pages to recycle it?"

Here's what you must realize: things have a life cycle. You may assume that an object's life cycle is forever, but it is not. The life cycle of a thing is measured by when it has completed its usefulness for you. Didn't the textbook train you as it needed to already? What more do you need from it?

The awkwardness you feel indicates the level of value the object has already brought to you. The only step remaining is to acknowledge its worth. You can honor the value it brought to you by expressing gratitude, "I'm so thankful for the knowledge this book brought me when I studied nursing. It's served its purpose for me, and I do not need to keep it anymore, but it has helped me to get to where I am now." You'd be amazed how speaking words of gratitude out loud (yes, out loud is best!) can give you permission to move on.

Our next category involves things you have been given by other people who are important to you or that you inherited from loved ones. These can be tricky because it may feel like you are disrespecting the relationship or that person's expectation of you by getting rid of it. Sometimes it seems like the spirit of that person is attached to the object and that by discarding the object, you discard the person. In these cases, it's best to evaluate whether you have something else from that person that both represents that person and is meaningful to you. You don't have to have fifty sort-of important things from someone when you have one that is significant. The best approach is to be ultra-selective. Let's look at the example of the beautiful coffee table book that you don't want, but feel like you should keep because your aunt gave it to you. Hold it in your hands and say, "I am grateful for the joy this brought my aunt, and I am excited for whoever finds this book at the library book sale and can enjoy it next." Isn't it better for the book to be in the hands of someone who will love it?

The final way that expressing gratitude helps with letting go is when you purchased something you thought you would use but didn't. Let's say you bought a very expensive series of books and CDs to learn French, and you never followed through. At that time, you really wanted to learn it, and take a trip to Paris. Instead, you took the trip to Paris and discovered you didn't have to know French after all. Now you no longer have the ambition to learn that language, which makes the expensive French course a buying mistake. How do you help yourself let go? You might say something like this, "I am so thankful to let go of my expectation that I will learn French. I've never been good at learning languages, and I'd rather spend my time in another way. Even though I have made a mistake in buying this, I am thankful to acknowledge that and be free." Speaking aloud your thankfulness for learning from a mistake may seem odd at first. Once you try it a few times, you may realize it allows you to move on. Why not give it a try?

Who Am I Without My Books?

Is Gwen still a teacher without her teaching materials? Is she still a book lover without physical books present in nearly every room? Having a physical representation of something intangible—such as intellectual knowledge—makes sense. It's a reflex to want to buy a souvenir when you go on a trip: it proves you went on the trip, it helps you remember it, and it feels like you have a piece of that place incorporated into yours. For Gwen, books and teaching materials were like Medals of Honor that show how she had spent her working life. Letting go of the physical reminders of her career could seem like she was diminishing the mark she left on the world. But is that really true?

Quantity is different than quality. If Gwen does nothing, her teaching materials will stay boxed up, and not enjoyed in the basement. The quantity actually served as a burdensome unfinished project. Once Gwen selectively chose a high-quality sample from her career to display, she could celebrate its value without having boxes and boxes of stuff.

When it came to books, Gwen discovered a shift in how she reads. She no longer devoured books for personal enjoyment or to prepare for teaching. Her newer habits revolved around reading for her book clubs, which greatly reduced the number of books she had to have. Gwen planned to join or start a book club after her move. The communal experience of books held more importance to her than the sheer number of books she owned.

Although Gwen joked that her memory wasn't what it used to be, her brain was still quite sharp. That sharpness would still exist even after releasing her book collection. Gwen could consider herself an intellectual and book lover regardless of how many or few books she possessed.

Getting the Project 100% Done

It helped that Gwen was giving the craft supplies, teaching games and tools to her old school. When she dropped them off, she could see that it would go to someone who would use them. Her other books would be sold to support the library, a cause dear to her heart. Finding specific recipients facilitates the process of letting things go because you know it benefits. Ask your friends for ideas about who might want certain things, but don't make the giving away process too complicated because it will really slow you down.

Gwen's donation recipients entailed two stops: her old school and her library. Gwen felt capable of following through. If she were to give the books on World War II to her friend who loves history, the music books to her niece, the art books to a local school, the children's books to her church, sell the paperbacks to the used books store, and send the old yearbooks to her high school, Gwen would quickly get overwhelmed. She would likely not follow through on the donation end of things, and her overall goals wouldn't be reached even though she had identified the books she no longer wanted.

Getting eighty-five percent done isn't the same as getting a hundred percent complete. If you are not getting to one hundred percent done, ask yourself if you can make the donation process less complicated by bringing it to just one or two places, by asking a friend to deliver donations for you, or by scheduling a pickup from a charitable donation center.

Gwen's Habit Action Plan

What needs to be done: Review how she acquires books.

What to do with it: Decide her new habits.

Where to start: At her new house.

When: After she has moved.

Who: Gwen.

Gwen will brainstorm the possibilities, which are:
- Borrow more print books from the library, which will require more planning ahead;
- Borrow more digital books from the library, which will require learning how to do that;
- Borrow books from her friends;

- Buy and download digital books to her tablet;
- Buy a print book, but consider having to then get rid of a book she already has as a one-in-one-out rule; and
- Buy a print book, but then pass it on to a friend.

Gwen saw herself using all of these possibilities. Most of all, Gwen wanted the physical books she owned to stay in balance at her new home. Her six-foot bookcase would signal her limit. Stacking books on top of other books or on top of the bookcase would not be allowed. To help reduce her acquisitions, she would follow these steps. Her first approach would be to borrow the book from the library, either as a print or digital copy. If she could not get it in time, she would buy the digital version. When she wanted to share a book with a friend, she would buy the print version. The fullness of the bookcase would give her a visual marker of how well her new habits were going.

Your Turn: Pause & Notice

- How many books do you own?
- Of that number, how many are yet to be read?
- How many will you re-read?
- What from Gwen's story resonated with you?
- Do you like the ambiance that books bring? How might you create a cozy feeling with fewer books?
- How could you continue to access new books or favorites without having to store the actual books?

- What action steps will you take around books? How about papers related to your profession?

Take photos of any grouping of books you have throughout your house, on shelves, by your nightstand, in a home office.

Discovery Questions

- Tell me about a time where you remember every detail of what happened: what you wore, who was there, the sounds, smells, and food. What makes this event stand out? Did things go as you expected?
- What relative are you most similar to? How so? In what ways is that good or bad? What can you learn from them on how to live or how not to live life?

CHAPTER 8

I Have to Get to That Closet!

*"Every thought, every emotion, is only a tourist. And I am not a hotel.
Let them come and let them go."*
Mooji

Barb's Story

Barb retired from thirty-three years as a bank loan officer with a closet full of suits, heels, coordinating purses, jewelry sets, and a drawer full of pantyhose. Barb's best friend Sue described her as "the most put-together woman she knows." Shortly after her divorce, Barb had a side business helping women style their clothes based on whether they had a spring, summer, fall, or winter skin tone.

Life was really hard for her in her early thirties. After an early marriage and staying home to care for her children, Barb's husband decided life with his secretary would be more exciting than with her. Barb managed to make ends meet by working as a bank teller and a Color Me Beautiful consultant. At first, she sewed her own suits, but later, as she worked her way up at the bank, she saved for higher-end "timeless" business wear. She did all this while trying to be both mother and father to her two kids.

Once her children were in college, she remarried. Life was good, and her children themselves found spouses and started families. Each special occasion was marked by a beautiful, carefully selected dress that still hung in the back of her closet. Back in the corner were a few boxes of hand-sewn children's clothes and Halloween costumes, markers of her creativity and thriftiness.

Since her retirement, Barb discovered a whole new set of stylish, but more casual, clothes. Her coffee group gals teased her about never wearing comfy clothes like they did. Barb suspected they were jealous that she hasn't gained weight like many of them have.

Barb's closet was packed so full that she bought a free-standing rack for her new clothes. She wasn't sure whether her husband's silence about the rack meant he didn't mind it. Her embarrassment about this dirty little secret kept her from hosting gatherings, in case anyone ventured into the bedroom. She intended to clean out and organize her closet but didn't get it done. She was too busy. It would take too long to try on all the clothes. She would do it when the season changed. And so, days passed, weeks passed, and still, she lived with a make-do solution.

Pause & Notice

- What problems does Barb see?
- What problems do others see?
- How did Barb's wardrobe benefit her in the past?
- What stands in the way of Barb doing things differently?
- What advice would you give Barb?

Barb's Tipping Point

PAIN OF REMAINING THE SAME	PAIN OF CHANGING	BENEFITS OF CHANGING
An unusable closet	Having to give away clothes that are too good for just donating	Having the clothes she wears now easily accessible to wear and put away
Having the hanging rack take up space in her bedroom	Knowing she's too sentimental, but not having an alternative	Not having to be reminded of her shortcomings every day when she sees the rack
Her husband feeling annoyed by the rack		Making herself and her husband happy by freeing up more bedroom space
Not having friends over because she's embarrassed		Having friends over again
Feeling not organized at home feels like a dirty little secret		Being proud of her home and feeling like she has nothing to hide
		Being free from this project that has been on her to do list for years

Visualize Success

- Success would look like a closet that includes only the clothes she liked to wear, that wasn't so crowded that it made her clothes wrinkled and that had room to store her clothes steamer. Success meant her bedroom would look proper again by not having a clothes rack against one wall.

- Success would feel like she had herself together and that she wasn't hiding anything. She would not have the stress of thinking she should be solving the problem. She would feel good when she walked into her bedroom and closet.

Barb's Project Action Plan

Goal: Have only the clothes she loves and that fit in her closet.

What needs to be done: Evaluate the clothes on her hanging rack and in the closet.

What to do with it: Keep what fits her life now, looks good, and is in good condition, and donate or discard the rest.

Where to start: With the clothing on the hanging rack, then the clothing in her closet.

When: Monday at 10 a.m.

Who: Barb and a professional organizer who was recommended by her best friend.

Barb will:

- Be honest about what she has or has not worn over the last year;

- Be willing to let go of items she doesn't love or that are damaged;

- Try on clothes to see if they still make her feel fashionable and attractive;

- Be willing to let go of items that were useful in an earlier time but that she does not wear now;

- Create a letting go process where they take a photo or talk about the importance of the memory clothes;

- Decide how she wants her closet arranged; and

- Feel proud of making so many decisions and of being able to help others by donating the clothes she does not wear.

The Organizer will:

- Hold up each piece of clothing and keep their focus on the hanging rack until it is complete;

- Ask Barb if she wears it and loves it;

- If yes, she places it back on the rack;

- If no, she takes it off the hanger and places it into a donation bag;

- Create a pile to try on and suggest Barb try things on once the pile has ten items;

- Get through the more current clothes, then move to the memory clothes;

- Help Barb take photos of the memory clothes;

- Listen if Barb feels like she needs to discuss the importance of those clothes; and

- Arrange the keep clothes into Barb's closet as Barb requests—by season, type, and color.

The Result

Barb didn't expect that she would feel so attached to the suits she wore during her career or the special occasion dresses. She decided to choose seven items of special significance to have made into a memory quilt. Taking photos of certain clothes before placing them in the donation bag also felt good. The organizer reminded her of the single moms out there who would be grateful to have her beautiful clothing available to them at a low cost. Barb felt better about letting the clothes go to a general donation place knowing that the right people could find her clothes there, even if she didn't see their faces when they chose the clothing. The process of going through the memory clothes reminded Barb of how resourceful she was during a very difficult time. She thought it would be worthwhile to write down the memories attached to the homemade children's clothing and Halloween costumes worn by her kids, and then give the clothing and a copy of the memories to them. She hoped that even if they didn't keep the clothing, that they could revisit some memories about wearing the pieces.

When Zombies Attack

Suit Yourself

More than once, I've heard people lament that their clothes that are too good for Goodwill, Salvation Army, or wherever. I don't think their hesitancy indicates that those places only deserve junky donations as much as it reflects the significance that they place on those particular items. The belief seems to be that because the items had extraordinary value for them, that there needs to be more pomp around letting go of them.

Giving designer clothing to a specific person allows someone to see the recipient's reaction. A personal exchange energizes both the giver and receiver—especially when the item appeals to a particular audience. For example, giving a model train collection to a child who collects model trains is much more fulfilling than dropping the set at the door of a charity store. But this desire must be balanced with the need to complete the process. It takes a lot of time and effort to deliver specific items to a specific audience. That effort should be saved for a handful of items, and the rest can be taken care of with a general donation. A process that drags on and on while looking for the perfect recipient is a recipe for frustration, often holding up the entire project.

If you find yourself in this situation, consider the following questions:

- What's so important about me knowing who receives these clothes next?
- What if I didn't have to control the part of the process where I know who gets it?
- What more do I need from this item?
- What will get me to my goal fastest?
- Do I need a letting go ritual?

Letting Go Rituals

When you think about it, most societies use rituals to mark transitions: baptisms, bar/bat mitzvahs, weddings, and funerals, just to name a few.

There's comfort in having a certain set of steps to mark a change. Creating a letting go ritual may be the missing link for you to move beyond that object and honor what it represents. Here are a few ideas, some of which Barb used.

Taking photos can be done with individual or grouped items. The photos can be made into a photo book through Shutterfly or Walgreens (and many other places, see chapter 10). This can be especially useful for a collection. Let's say you are a master quilter with a quilt collection too big to keep. Before you begin to give away or sell your quilts, you can create a record of your creative masterpieces so that even when you don't possess the actual quilt, you have the memory of that particular project in a very compact form.

Journaling the object's history or significance can be done separately or in conjunction with a photo. You can easily journal a bit about each photo in a digital photo book. But if making a digital book feels overwhelming, you can print a photo, tape it to a piece of paper, then handwrite a description underneath it. The paper goes into a vinyl page protector in a three-ring binder. Voilà. You have your own memory album of special things without having to keep the objects.

People are sometimes frustrated that their loved ones—especially their children—aren't interested in hearing the history of an object, let's say a figurine you purchased on a trip to Ireland twenty years ago. Tell me, why are you mystified that they don't want to hear about it if they did not go on the trip with you? I don't mean to be insensitive, but the figurine is *your* souvenir from *your* memorable trip. It does not have to have the same meaning to someone else to be considered valuable to your life story. The most important aspect of this is for you to tell that story, regardless of whether the audience extends beyond you.

Your children might appreciate the significance of the story at a later time. Let's say the figurine replicates an angel from the Irish cathedral special to your family because it's where their great-grandmother was baptized before they immigrated to America. When your negligent children find your journal and realize how wrong they were to not listen to you, you can jump with glee from your vantage point at the pearly gates of Heaven. For now, though, writing that history will be valuable to you as you sift through your life's legacy.

Sentimental items can be honored and enjoyed in a new form. Surely, you've seen the quilts made from sports t-shirts worn during a student school years. You can make (or have made) a concert t-shirt quilt. Create a pillow from your deceased father's neckties. Design a shadow box from your grandfather's Purple Heart medal or your daughter's favorite childhood dress and toys. My children treasure the teddy bears made from their favorite uncle's clothes after he died. Your imagination poses the only limit to what can be turned into a visible and enjoyable memory object. And even that can be supplemented by a plethora of ideas found on pinterest.com.

I'll wear it once I lose fifteen pounds

How much dust has gathered on your "wish" clothing? Wish clothing refers to clothes you *wish* you could wear. Do you know how much time has passed since you set your ambitious intention? Maybe you have different levels of wish clothing—fifteen pounds, twenty-five pounds, and forty pounds—all of which are diminishing the functionality of your closet. Think about how often a person uses his or her closet. It's every day, right? Every single day you add stress to getting dressed. Barb put a bandage on this problem by buying a hanging clothes rack to hang her current clothes, which caused other problems.

Everyone should be able to trust her closet. That means going to your closet and knowing that everything in front of you fits, feels good to wear, is in good condition, and has been worn in the last year. Can you imagine how calm you would feel to know that you want to wear every single piece of clothing in your closet? The stress of getting ready would be gone.

What stands in the way of you having a closet you can trust? It really comes down to your ability to make good decisions. Good decisions require awareness of who you are now. If that person weighs 185 pounds, then don't try to fit into clothes meant for someone who is 150 pounds. You will look better in clothes that fit your body. You will feel more confident. Every day that you squeeze into clothes that don't fit is a day you remind yourself that you aren't good enough. Every time you see the shirts that don't fit you now, you confirm that you aren't acceptable until you have lost weight.

Good decisions involve testing the things you tell yourself. Let's look at some of the reasons why people keep clothes they shouldn't (check all that apply to you):

- ❏ It doesn't quite fit right, but it mostly fits. I'll just wear it around the house.
- ❏ I can hide the holes if I wear it under a sweater.
- ❏ It was on sale, and I didn't feel like trying it on there. When I found out it didn't fit, I never took it back. I guess I'll just keep it.
- ❏ It's out of style now, but fashions always come back around.

- ❑ I'll probably wear that this season.
- ❑ I'll never wear this again, but I spent so much on that dress that I better hold on to it.
- ❑ These are perfectly good blazers, although I am not sure when I would wear them.

What reasons you would add? Did any of the above statement make you laugh because you've said them? Expressing your unconscious thoughts—no matter how silly—by speaking or writing them helps you to uncover the rules you have been living by. Once you uncover your unspoken rules, you can consciously choose what rules to keep, which don't fit your life, and create new ones that align. We interpret the discomfort felt during a decision to mean we should stop the process. However, when the process halts because you are worried about making a bad decision, you return to avoiding the project. The opposite approach will get you unstuck. Instead of thinking the discomfort means stop, regard the discomfort as a sign to get more information via truth-testing techniques.

Truth-Testing Techniques

If you really believe you will fit into your wish clothes, then truth-test your claim. Find a good-sized box. Pull all the clothes from your closet that are one size too small. Make a donation pile for the clothes that you don't like. Set aside clothes that hold special memories. Be really selective with what you keep in this category. Memory clothes should be placed in their own bin. Return to the too-small clothes and place them in the box. Set a date—it can be a year from now—and write it on the outside flap of the box. That's the box's expiration date. If that date arrives and you aren't well on your way to wearing those clothes, take them directly to donation. Do not open the box! You will undermine your progress. By pulling out the memory clothes at the onset, you know there is nothing in the box that you can't live without. You have lived without it for a year already and who knows how long before that. A tested truth will set you free from a fuzzy truth, free to have a closet you can trust. One more note, clothes more than one size too small should be donated automatically. If you must, you can duplicate the process and place an expiration date of eighteen months on these. Or, make good decisions now and be done with it.

Another truth-testing technique is called the backward hanger test. I don't know who came up with this idea. I first heard it from organizing guru, Peter Walsh. Here's how it works: Turn all your hangers with the hook facing towards you, rather than the normal way of facing towards the back of the closet. Warning: your arm may get tired reaching up to switch the hanger orientation. Once this step is done, and all hangers are facing the opposite direction, you will evaluate what you actually do wear because each time you wear something, you'll launder it and hang it up with the hanger the normal way. Over time it will be easy to see what you actually use or don't use. At that time—I recommend six months—simply pull what you don't wear off the backward hanger into a donation bag, and send it away. The ten minutes it took to turn the hangers backward saved the more active process of deciding by piece.

Barb's Habit Action Plan

What needs to be done: Create a new flow for her clothing purchases.

What to do with it: Follow the one-in-one-out rule where every time she buys a new piece of clothing, she will let go of a piece of clothing. That way she will keep the closet in balance with her current clothing.

Where to start: Barb will write "one-in-one-out" on an index card and tape it to the wall in her closet.

When: Next time she shops for herself.

Who: Barb and her husband.

Barb will:

- Ask her husband to remind her for the next two months of her reminder card just one time on the evening of the day she buys new clothes.

Barb's husband will:

- Remind Barb just once, and as requested, and not expand it into nagging.

Your Turn: Pause & Notice

- What memory clothes do you have?
- Are you keeping your memory clothes hidden away because you don't know what else to do with them?
- Would you follow through on making those memory clothes into something you would enjoy more frequently?

- What are your rules for deciding what to keep in your closet?

- Does everything in your closet fit? Feel good to wear?

- What from Barb's story resonated with you?

- What action steps will you take around your clothing?

Take photos of the closets where you store your clothes.

Discovery Questions

- If you had to choose a different career, what would it be, and why?

- What object in your home is a discussion starter?

- What should you probably throw away, but you kind of want to keep anyway?

CHAPTER 9

Mr. Fix-it to the Rescue

"Part of our conflict with controlling people is that we tend to fight them for the very thing they won't surrender."
David Solie

John's Story

All of John's neighbors knew who to call with their tricky electrical issues. John's church knew who to call. John's extended family knew who to call. The church office made a sweatshirt that said "Mr. Fix-it to the Rescue" as a thank you gift for his work on a major project. The fifteen-year-old sweatshirt was frayed and faded but still worn proudly.

John broke his hip while cleaning out his house gutters. Thankfully, a neighbor spotted him, and helped him. In the year since his wife died, John's children repeatedly told him it was time to move and that it was definitely time to hire others to do anything that involved a ladder. If John hadn't had to go to the hospital, he would have never let his kids have the satisfaction of saying "I told you so."

He managed to return home after surgery and a stint in a rehabilitation center. John could mostly manage daily living, but it was hard to go to his workshop in the basement or to the upstairs bedrooms. He wasn't about to tell his kids the truth about how much he couldn't do. They had pestered him enough about moving. "There are some people who do okay moving to the old folk's home," he told them, "And there are some people who move and die."

When his daughter Sandy, came to visit, she could tell by the dust on the second floor and in the basement that he wasn't using more than three or four rooms on the main floor. John wouldn't discuss it. "I'm still recovering from surgery," he told her. "I have plenty of projects I want to finish down there. Just leave my stuff alone!"

Not long after that, John's family staged an intervention. Under the excuse of a "fun Labor Day weekend," his four adult children showed up and told him they were cleaning out the basement whether he liked it or not and that the dumpster was arriving in the morning. John was not pleased. His face got red and he told them to butt out.

"But you don't need those tools!" said the son who set up the intervention.

"I sure do," replied John. "Everyone knows how handy I am. What will the church do? What will Mrs. Jones next door do if she needs something fixed?"

"When's the last time you helped someone? Five years ago?" John's son was fuming now too. He had flown in from out of town to take care of this problem. "They need to hire someone else. You've done your duty."

"It was more recent than that," said John. "At least I think it was."

John stalked off to his bedroom and closed the door. He wasn't sure what to do or how to feel. Part of him knew his kids loved him and part of him was angry, and maybe a little scared. How did they know what was important to him? What if he wanted to keep his tools and do his projects? Why should they be the ones to decide?

Pause & Notice

- What problems does John see?

- What problems do others see?

- How was John successful in the past?

- What stands in the way of John doing things differently?

- What advice would you give John?

John's Tipping Point

PAIN OF REMAINING THE SAME	PAIN OF CHANGING	BENEFITS OF CHANGING
Being pressured by his kids	Having to give up his belongings, especially his tools	Kids will stop pestering him and will know he is safe
Knowing that there are things in the house he should get rid of	Having to make tough decisions	If others help, he doesn't have to do it himself
	Letting his family help means he won't have control over the process	He won't burden his kids with having to do it later
	Not being able to have the tools on hand to help people	
	Feeling like he is old and useless	

Visualize Success

- John cannot imagine any version of success related to downsizing his home. His version of success would be to get his kids to leave him alone so he could continue as he was. While he knew he had changed physically, his goal of staying in his home of many years and continuing to be active and useful had not changed.

- His children viewed success as making John see that he was making poor choices. They wanted to move him to a more physically safe environment. Because he was minimizing the physical risks, they did not see his goal of aging in place as realistic.

- These two visions of success were at odds and guaranteed conflict.

Step into Action?

This was a tricky, and not uncommon, situation. John was not a willing participant in the process. His adult children wanted what was best for their widower father, who they believed may be at risk of getting hurt. Since John had full cognitive capacity, by law, his children couldn't force him to do anything. The tug-of-war could negatively affect John, his relationship with his children, and their relationship with each other as they argued about what to do.

At the heart of John's internal struggle was not being able to see that the future has anything to hold for him. How can Mr. Fix-it survive if he didn't have his tools? His tools were his means of connecting with others. When his wife died, John became more isolated. Because John had difficulty expressing his feelings, his children hadn't considered the impact of getting rid of his tools, let alone the daunting idea that he would move. They felt impatient with his seeming inability to admit there was a problem. The solution of downsizing and moving seemed pretty clear to them. They saw John's resistance as stubbornness and selfishness. John saw their involvement as over-reactionary and interfering.

The family needed an outside perspective, someone whom John trusts. Fortunately, a friend from church, Tom, fit the bill. Tom served on several committees with John and was a Stephen Minister—a program that trained church members on providing one-on-one confidential care during difficult times. Sandy got her father's permission to contact Tom to set up a meeting with the three of them. As a former drug and alcohol counselor, Tom was also familiar with a concept called "harm reduction" that identified ways to lessen a situation's greatest risks rather than address the entire issue. For example, harm reduction for an I.V. drug user meant receiving clean needles to minimize contracting H.I.V. or other diseases caused by sharing needles. Let's look at how harm reduction might look for John's situation.

A Harm Reduction Project Action Plan

Goal: To increase John's safety while he continues to age in place.

What needs to be done: Identify the top risk areas; rebuild trust in the relationship by using better communication techniques and Tom as a mediator.

What to do with it: Negotiate ways to minimize the safety risks.

Where to start: Garage.

When: Sunday at 2 p.m.

Who: John, daughter Sandy, and church friend Tom.

Tom will:

- Begin by having a conversation with John;
- Not touch any of John's things;
- Not give John advice;
- Reminisce about times John helped at the church;
- Reinforce John's values of helping others and sharing knowledge;
- Ask John if he knows of any school or youth groups or vocational programs that need mentors who are electrical experts;
- Brainstorm ways John can share his talents with them;
- Ask Sandy to share her concerns about safety issues in the home;
- Ask John to restate Sandy's concerns in his own words; and
- Start to explore solutions to reduce the safety risks (i.e., agree to call someone to help if the task requires getting on a ladder).

John will:

- Be open to talking with Tom and Sandy;
- Consider options to use his talents in different ways;
- Restate what he hears are his daughter's concerns;
- Acknowledge the possible risks;
- Express what he desires to happen; and
- Come to an agreement on what he is willing to do to reduce the risks (i.e., hire people to clean his gutters or fix things that require a ladder).

Sandy will:

- Resist the urge to interrupt Tom and her father;
- Be patient about not addressing the safety issues until later;
- Acknowledge her father's right to self-determine and treat him as a competent adult (rather than think of him as feeble-minded);
- Express her heartfelt concerns for her father's safety as the most important reason she is hoping for a change;
- Focus on safety issues and not bring up the additional need to downsize the upstairs and basement right now; and
- Affirm her father for being willing to have the conversation.

When Zombies Attack

Who Decides What is Best?

When a loved one appears to be making poor choices, you naturally want to fix the problem. But what is the problem? Is it his poor choices or is something else driving his behaviors? And who determines the problem and the solutions? The surface behavior often has served some purpose, even if that behavior causes additional problems. If you have eaten potato chips in front of the television to ease your loneliness, drank wine to take the edge off a stressful day, or went shopping to distract yourself from an upsetting situation, then you have followed the same behavior pattern of the loved one whom you perceive to be in danger. The degree of severity may be less, but the pattern is the same.

From outside a situation, the solution looks obvious. Being too fat is solved by eating less and moving more. Consuming too much alcohol means drinking less or stopping altogether. Over-shopping is fixed by not going to stores in person or online. How about having too much stuff? That's resolved simply by getting rid of your clutter, right? Thank goodness I could fix your problem by giving you the solution. Wait—I didn't?

Finding solutions for what ails you includes two parts: self-awareness that a problem exists; and an alternative reaction to the stressor. Someone may consciously or unconsciously realize there is an issue, but not see an alternative way to manage the situation. The stimulus and response are deeply embedded. If you have depended upon alcohol to release built-up stress, then just taking it away without a replacement release behavior will probably not work. Change requires a willingness by the person affected to try something different.

Resisting Change

Recall a time when you gave someone advice, and all he or she gave back to you were reasons why it couldn't work. Resistance to change is a natural reaction. If you don't believe me, take this book over to someone near you. Place it in their hands, allow them to get a firm grip, and then try to take it from them. Their instinct is to grab it back. They may not even know what they are grabbing back, but they do know you are trying to take something away. The most effective way to motivate change is to get the person to argue for his own change. Motivational Interviewing (M.I.) is an evidence-based technique designed to do just this.

When people are ambivalent—or unsure—about whether or not they want to change, they delay taking action. Because they have mixed desires, they feel conflicted, and that causes anxiety. Anxiety leads to avoidance. Motivational

Interviewing can resolve ambivalence and spark a person's own motivation to change. M.I. can be applied to many situations, from helping a person consistently take her medication to help her deal with an addiction. Find out more about Motivational Interviewing at https://motivationalinterviewing.org/.

A Motivational Interviewing practitioner partners with the client in the process, accepting the client's perspective, strengths, and ability to make his own decisions. The practitioner expresses compassion for the client, always holding his best interest in mind, as well as believing that the client is the best expert on himself. This means that the client generates the best ideas. The partnering done in M.I. makes a client to feel welcome and understood, creating a trusting relationship that becomes the center of productive work. John had lost trust with his children, so the hopes of finding mutual goals became nearly impossible. When Tom, who was skilled in M.I. techniques, stepped in to create trust, it opened the situation to engage multiple perspectives again. Tom could then focus the conversation towards John talking about change, rather than resisting it. From there, they could move towards making a plan.

All Interventions Carry Risks

Just as there are risks to having someone continue to live in an unsafe environment, there are risks to intervening. The primary principle of harm reduction, according to Patt Denning, is to do no harm, meaning that the way you are helping should not cause more harm than the person's actual behavior causes. If John was suffering from Hoarding Disorder, doing a clean-out without his permission could have very negative consequences that range from feeling so assaulted that he refuses contact with anyone associated with the clean-out to continuing to re-hoard any space he lives into losing his desire to live.

Similar to Motivational Interviewing, Harm Reduction begins by building trust and treating the person as an expert on herself. As a contributing team member—not just as a blockade—the person needing help assists in coming up with solutions. She may have an idea that no one else has considered. The fact that it came from her increases the likelihood that she will follow through with it. All people involved in a Harm Reduction process need to feel like valuable and competent members of the team. M.I. techniques are often used in harm reduction.

Additional things to know about a Harm Reduction approach are that change can be slow. The benefit of slow change is that it allows a person to adjust gradually rather than be forced to make quick changes that don't last. The slow pace also accommodates the inevitable backsliding that can occur as changes get implemented. When someone reverts to doing things the old way—which is called backsliding—it's an opportunity to tweak the new behaviors to function better. You can improve functionality by examining roadblocks and troubleshooting solutions. Perhaps the new system can be reduced by one or two steps if it is too hard to maintain. If you are helping someone who has slipped into old habits, how you react will set the tone for the reaction of the person who is backsliding. Convey support and reaffirm the original agreement rather than relying on shame and blame.

When is it Hoarding?

People throw around the word "hoarder" to mean anything from having a messy room to a person who is sentimental to someone who collects things.

Awareness about hoarding behaviors has increased because of the television show, *Hoarders*, and programs like it. These shows have been a double-edged sword in that they raise awareness and compassion at the same time as reinforcing the shame of hoarding, treating the condition like a car wreck to be gawked at. In 2012, hoarding shifted from being treated as a sub-category of Obsessive-Compulsive Disorder to being its own diagnosable condition. Researchers are working hard to find better treatments for people who hoard and relief for the loved ones impacted by hoarding behaviors. It's a very complex condition, often related to unprocessed trauma. A common mistake loved ones make is trying to get the person who hoards to change by reasoning with him. To find out more about how to treat Hoarding Disorder, I recommend reading *Digging Out: Helping Your Loved One Manage Clutter, Hoarding, and Compulsive Acquiring* (Tompkins, 2009).

Saving and collecting things are behaviors that fall on a continuum. Some people have created paperless, minimalist lives, and others have kept every check stub going back decades. If your stuff is impacting your life so that you cannot function in rooms as they are intended (cook in the kitchen, wash up in the bathroom, sleep in the bedroom) or causes crippling debt, fractured relationships, and other equally negative impacts, you may be affected by hoarding behaviors. But it may also be something else. That's why it is so important to get a diagnosis from a qualified mental health practitioner. You may have depression, PTSD, a thyroid issue, or simply haven't learned the process of letting go. Knowing which condition, if any, will help to find the right treatment or set of treatments.

If you suspect a loved one is affected by Hoarding Disorder, the best thing you can do is educate yourself. Read *Digging Out,* or another of the helpful books available. Don't initiate or participate in a clear-out that will harm a loved one more than help her. Help the loved one get support from therapists who are familiar with Motivation Interviewing, Harm Reduction, Cognitive-Behavioral Therapy, and Hoarding Disorder.

Having a collection that is displayed with pride and that doesn't interfere with daily functioning is probably not hoarding disorder. Keeping one box of letters from your deceased parent differs from having a room full of things from your deceased parent. I cannot tell you for sure whether you have hoarding behaviors. I can direct you to resources related to that. Throughout this book, I have presented techniques for learning how to let go, which may be helpful if you lean more towards the collecting side of the saving spectrum.

New Ways for John to Feel Valuable

We all want to feel valued throughout our lives, not just when we are young and healthy. When someone is not physically able to do tasks that have brought him joy or allowed him to serve others, the loss is significant. To respond to clients in this situation, I listen deeply and ask myself these questions:

- What aspects of this situation has the person enjoyed the most?
- What aspects does he or she not care as much about?
- How could the most enjoyable parts be adapted in a new form?

If John had a new outlet to share his talents, he could still feel valuable without doing the parts that are better for him not to do (such as climbing ladders or hauling heavy items). Explore the possibilities. Are there Boy or Girl Scout troops who do projects related to John's expertise? Could he mentor an Eagle Scout? Could he teach an adult class at the local community college on how to fix things around the home? Perhaps the vocational skills teacher at the local high school knows of ways John could share his knowledge. Additional benefits of John connecting with others include him feeling less isolated, as well as lighting the spark that comes from intergenerational interaction. The young people he teaches may help him learn new technologies, the latest slang, and remind him of what it's like to be sixteen. A shift like this invites new blessings rather than clinging to what has been lost.

Compassion, patience, and openness to building trust are at the heart of making John's difficult situation better. Bringing in someone skilled to mediate the situation moves a tense stand-off into a viable partnership for moving forward. The conversations may still prove difficult, but at least they honor the needs of those involved.

John's Habit Action Plan

What needs to be done: Avoid using ladders.

What to do with it: Get someone else to do the task involving ladders.

Where and When to start: Next time John needs a repair on the outside of the house, to access the attic, paint, or another task that requires a ladder.

Who: John can call Tom, choose another service provider on his own, ask Sandy to help with the task or with finding a helper. Perhaps the members of the youth or vocation group will help John in exchange for his involvement with the group.

John will:

- Honor his agreement to call someone else when the task involves ladders;
- Seek help from Tom or Sandy with the task or to find service providers; and
- Find alternatives to accomplish some tasks that need a ladder, such as buying a long arm light bulb changer or other reaching tools.

Sandy will:

- Praise her father for honoring their agreement;
- Promptly respond to her father's requests for help;
- Kindly redirect her father to their agreement if he breaks it; and
- Ask Tom to mediate again if John continues to break the agreement.

Your Turn: Pause & Notice

- Do you still climb on ladders for home projects?
- Is this a risk you should take? What do others say?
- How often do you use your tools right now?
- What tools or other possessions represent who you are or have been?
- What from John's story resonated with you?
- What action steps will you take around your tools? Your garage?

- If you have a similar situation going on with a loved one, what options might improve your communication and create a better outcome?

Take a photo of your tools or things in your garage.

Discovery Questions

- What are your biggest fears about your health?
- When have you been quite sick in the past? How did you get through that illness?
- If you had $50,000 available to give to a person or a charity, where would you donate it? Why would they be worthy recipients?

CHAPTER 10

Time to Make the Scrapbooks

*"All that you are seeking is also seeking you. If you sit still, it will find you.
It has been waiting for you a long time."*
Clarissa Pinkola Estés

Bethany's Story

Bethany loved being a mom to her three kids, who were all out of college except for the youngest. If her kids were involved in an activity, you could find her volunteering. Over the twenty years before her youngest graduated high school, she was the class mom, the Boy Scouts den mom, Girl Scout leader, as well as coordinator for the girls' soccer meals and events, class trip chaperone, Parent's Club president, library aide, and more. She took pride in the fact that the kids hung out at her home. She could produce a meal for fifteen teens at the drop of a hat. She was a second mom to many of her kids' friends. When her kids left for college, she missed their friends, too. Since Rachel, her youngest, went to college, Bethany avoided the deafening quiet of her house.

Bethany planned to use her "empty nest" time finally catching up on scrapbooking memories from her kids' childhood activities and the plethora of photos that had collected in boxes and on her laptop. She had all the supplies: empty scrapbooks, packets of colorful paper, expensive stickers related to specific sports, and plenty of general stickers, too. A few years ago, her husband helped her set up a scrapbook room in her basement complete with cabinets, decorative bins, organizers for her supplies, and a fancy work table. It looked like something out of a magazine. She began a scrapbook for Noah, the oldest, and Naomi, her middle child.

When her children were born, she set the intention of making one book per year, per child. Life with young children was too busy to work on scrapbooks, so she shifted her focus to just collecting each child's school papers, awards, and photos in larger bins in the scrapbook room. She frequently complained to Rachel about not getting the scrapbooks done. But she stopped complaining when she caught Rachel throwing away her high school papers before leaving for college. Bethany didn't trust that her children yet knew what was worthy of saving.

At that point, Bethany redefined her goal yet again. She saw her next step as sorting the kids' papers into boxes by year. She made it about one-third of the way into getting Noah's papers sorted when she gave up. The scrapbook room actually looked worse than when she had started. Piles teetered on any available counter space and parts of the floor. Yet-to-be-filled specialty boxes reached to the ceiling. New supplies, still in store bags, gathered in a small mountain next to the door, where she had tossed them in.

Noah brought home his girlfriend and wanted to show her a few photos of himself as a baby. He took her into the scrapbooking room to find them. The shame of having someone outside of the family see her disorganized room was too much for Bethany. Despite wanting to make a good impression on Noah's new girlfriend, Bethany found herself shouting at her son. Since then, Noah had been giving Bethany the cold shoulder, and she felt sick about it.

She resolved to get the room sorted no matter what. But every time she looked into the room she quickly left. Where in the world would she start?

Pause & Notice

- What problems does Bethany see?
- What problems do others see?
- What life changes may be affecting Bethany?
- Could Bethany accomplish her goals differently?
- What stands in the way of Bethany doing things differently?
- What advice would you give Bethany?

Bethany's Tipping Point

PAIN OF REMAINING THE SAME	PAIN OF CHANGING	BENEFITS OF CHANGING
Not being able to enjoy completed scrapbooks	Having to get past feeling overwhelmed to get started	Easily looking back on memories with her kids
Having the undone projects hanging over her head	Acknowledging how much time it will take	Not feeling burdened by the projects
Having a messy scrapbook room	Being unsure if she wants to take all that time	Having something manageable to look at that isn't in boxes
Being unable to find pictures she wants to find	If she alters her goal, does that mean she wasted her money on materials?	Having an organized space to use for future scrapbooking

Feeling disappointed in herself	If she never starts, she cannot fail	Feeling proud of herself for following through
Feeling like she's letting down the kids	Is having scrapbooks something the kids even care about?	Feeling like a good mom
	Can she scrapbook all the kids' stuff evenly, so no one feels jealous?	

Visualize Success

- Success would look like having each child's growing up years organized into memory books that could be enjoyed. They would be able to easily find photos and memories from each year. Success would look like an orderly craft room.

- Success would feel like taking action rather than procrastinating. Success would mean she was following through on her values to honor her family members by helping them to keep their memories.

Bethany's Project Action Plan

What needs to be done: Organize Bethany's memory papers/photos of her kids.

What to do with it: Get clear on her end goal, and then create a method for deciding what to keep or not keep.

Where to start: By picking up on the system that Bethany started of sorting by child.

When: Tuesday at 10 a.m.

Who: Bethany and a photo organizing specialist, who can be found at the Association of Personal Photo Organizers: https://www.appo.org.

Bethany will:

- Describe why and how she would like to create memory books;
- Consider multiple options for achieving the end goal and chose the one that makes the most sense for what she is able to do;
- Make guidelines for what she wants to keep or not;
- Set up the staging area; and
- Make decisions as the organizer hands her papers.

The Photo Organizer will:

- Ask Bethany questions about her end goal, including finding out why Bethany is so committed to her plan for making the scrapbooks in that way;
- Ask questions about Bethany's previous approach to see how that can still serve her goals or how it may need to change;
- Find out what types of papers Bethany most wants to keep and which can be discarded;
- Set up the space to have a clear staging area to reduce overwhelm;
- Presort school papers by child as much as possible so Bethany can make decisions on what to keep; and
- Gather what is kept into chronological order.

Bethany and the photo organizer were able to make great progress in clearing up the center of the room. Bethany no longer felt overwhelmed by the area because the sorting system operated like an assembly line. On the main workbench, there were legal sized plastic bins for each child, with file folders labeled by grade. Next to each bin were loose papers to be decided on. Some of the papers were already sorted by kid, others were mixed. They were not seeking to be meticulous at this stage, just to pile papers next to the correct bin.

A large garbage can make it easy to discard unwanted papers. As they came across bags with supplies, they sorted them into general areas: stickers, rubber stamps, and papers, to be further organized later. Aside from school photos, which were placed with that child's bin, other photos were collected in boxes in one area to figure out later. It was clear to Bethany that this might take a lot more time than she realized, and while she was happy with making real progress, she was also reconsidering the scope of her plans.

When Zombies Attack

Photographs: A Blessing and a Curse

Photos are a wonderful thing, except when they aren't. Gone are the days of waiting breathlessly for your photos to return from the developers, wondering if there were any good ones, knowing that you paid for developing every print, whether blurry or clear. Often you ordered doubles of each print so that you could share the good ones. Rarely did the bad ones or extras get thrown out. The prints were placed on a desk for a while until the developer envelope was placed in a box in a closet. In some households, prints were anchored with photo corners onto peachy paper sheets inside a black-covered photo book. Later those books were replaced by "magnetic" albums, where you pulled back the clear acetate protector and placed photos wherever you wanted on the adhesive-backed pages. Over time, these album pages turned yellow, the acidic adhesive damaging the photos within. Slide-in albums that fit the now-standard size of four-by-six inches came next. These albums fit three photos to a page, or six.

During the slide era—the late 1950s through the mid-1990s—color positive film was developed into 35mm slides. The small transparencies fit into two-by-two-inch slide mounts which slotted into a circular carousel. On Saturday nights, a family might gather in a darkened room, listening as the slide projector hummed and the carousel clicked forward as a new image illuminated the blank wall. They reminisced about trips and holidays while eating popcorn and staying up a little too late.

Slide carousels got stored in square cardboard boxes next to the boxes holding black and white prints, and color prints of various sizes from various times. Maybe some albums were stored in the closet too, or out on a shelf in the living room. Sometimes people looked through the photo albums, but rarely did the carousels come out after the nineteen-seventies passed.

The first digital camera debuted in 1975 and became widely popular in the late 1990s. The technology of single lens reflex (SLR) cameras made it easier for non-experts to take good photos. Digital cameras allowed users to take as many photos as desired because they could see which ones turned out and which didn't. People still made prints from photo files, but less so.

Now, every smartphone has a camera more powerful than most of the original technologies. Rather than print photos, people share them on social media. Another option is to view them on a digital frame like Nixplay, which allows anyone with access to the account to send photos to the frame, making it a great solution for widely dispersed family members. Photo files make it easy to create albums, products like pillows, canvas prints, and much more. Some services, like Chatbooks.com, print photo books automatically from your phone. Digitized photos allow you to tag and search photos, and face recognition software can help to organize digital photos. Some drawbacks to everyone having a smartphone that takes photos are that bad photos don't get deleted, making digital disorganization the new struggle, as well as people neglecting to back up photos or to delay printing them.

What about those dusty boxes of print photos and slide carousels? These can be digitized and shared, too. Some ways are more cumbersome and expensive than others. Like other societal shifts from scarcity to plenty, photos have become easy to take and view, which can be a good and a bad thing. A hundred years ago, you might have one photo of siblings at a family reunion; now, you might have photos of what was on each sibling's plate.

With such an abundance of photos, your best tool is discernment. Does it make sense to keep everything? How does having so much interfere with being able to enjoy what you have? The "less is more" philosophy applies here. Do I need to see twenty pictures of Johnny eating spaghetti for the first time or just the best two? Making those decisions takes time. There's more to process and weed out. And that's just to narrow down the best photos of one day's event. How many more days and events are there? No wonder it is so overwhelming.

I remember my Mom having pervasive guilt about photos. She intended to place our photos into slide-in albums, but first, she had to organize the photo backlog into chronological order. That task was so overwhelming that she never did it—and it was only two boxes! The number of photos that I have taken of my kids is in the thousands. These photos are a combination of developed and digital. My print photos are arranged chronologically in slide-in books, and my digital photo files are automatically placed by date. My generation expects themselves to produce something additional for each child that tells the story of his or her life. How much more involved is this project? What does it mean about you as a Mom or Dad if you are able to put together such a memory book? What does it mean about your parenting if you do not have memories organized? Where did this expectation come from anyway?

As parents die, their children inherit unorganized boxes of photos (which are overwhelming to dig in to) or organized albums (which seem disrespectful to disassemble and divide). These inherited photos may bring joy, and they may bring a deep burden. You know the photos show extended family members, but you don't know their names. You may know who, but you don't know the date or location. Worst of all, not knowing may not matter to you. Here is the crux of the matter. Does not wanting to track these things make you a negligent child? It's really up to you to decide how you will spend your time. If you are able, try to get details on important family photos before your elders die. Even then, your efforts may not bear fruit. An audience member in one of my presentations explained how she attempted to get her Mom to write who was in her photos and when they were taken. "It didn't help much," she said, "because Mom just wrote things like 'Us. Last year'."

What assumptions are you making when you think about organizing photos? A major one is that you must keep them. Another one is that you are supposed to turn the photos into something that can be enjoyed by the family. It's like you have been voted to be the family historian, a role you may or may not want. Even if you do want to be the family historian, you have permission to define the project on your terms. Some options to lighten the load include using LegacyBox, ScanCafe, and ScanMyPhotos to digitize and share the most important photographs. Also, you can hire someone to help you by going to the Association of Personal Photo Organizers at https://www.appo.org.

Family Values

Bethany had strong opinions that she should create scrapbooks for each of her children that included photos of them and their childhood papers. She assumed that she should do it because that's what good moms did. Bethany grew up in a home with an unsentimental mother who didn't keep much of anything. On the one hand, Bethany knew her desire to keep memories stemmed from her own opposite experience. On the other hand, Bethany could not gauge what were reasonable expectations for memorabilia projects. As long as she kept her assumptions unexamined, her project expectations would be out of balance.

One thing was crystal clear to Bethany: she didn't want to act like her mother when it came to saving things. She wanted her children to know that they were special, that their histories were important to her, and that what they made along the way was worth keeping. Because her only other model was her mother keeping nothing, Bethany's default model had been to keep everything. If Bethany had the assistance of a therapist (which I believe everyone can benefit from having), then she could process her either-or-thinking and see how much her drive to save memories for her children might be connected to trying to heal a hurt part of herself. The irony of Bethany's overly complicated expectations was that her children didn't have accessible memory books either. What she said she so desperately wanted to provide was not being delivered.

Bethany wanted to achieve the outcome of making her family members feel special. In her mind, Bethany saw herself and her children sitting side-by-side on a sofa, looking at photos and papers from their childhoods. They would be laughing at good memories and sharing stories about other memories, and most of all, feeling connected. Memory books could remind them of the details of those shared memories. In an ideal world, her children would express appreciation for how those books were put together, but at the very least, Bethany herself would treasure how the books have created a sense of togetherness.

If the overall aim is to experience togetherness, then how complicated do the memory books need to be? Does every milestone need to be identified? Will the pages need to be laid out aesthetically, with no scrapbook page being the same or can it be simpler than that? Perhaps togetherness could be nurtured by keeping only the photos that fit in a medium box, and the box could be brought out for occasional viewing. The time investment in the paper scrapbook option could easily be ten times the time investment of culling memories down into a box. Many options between these two are possible. Ask yourself, "How much time am I willing to spend on this?" and "Who expects that particular product?" Bethany's children may not be attached to the idea of having a fancy memory book. Their best outcome may be just to have easy access to the memories.

Adapting to a Different Approach

Bethany has had a certain approach to memory-making in mind for a very long time. She didn't feel comfortable abandoning her plan to make paper scrapbooks and to meticulously organize all the photos chronologically. But she also knew that her previous plan was probably too much. She felt tied to the old plan because she had purchased so many supplies for paper scrapbooks. See Chapter 2 for managing buying mistakes.

She had never made a digital photo book and wondered if she would like that. The technology piece felt a little intimidating to her even though she was generally familiar with computers and navigating the internet. A good experiment for Bethany would be to try making a digital photo book. By framing it as an experiment, the stakes remained low, and her options stayed open. Choosing a recent subject matter that was already digitized—such as last year's Christmas photos—and using different resources to learn how to do it could reduce overwhelm as well. I've detailed below how Bethany might complete that experiment as a Habit Action Plan.

Bethany's Habit Action Plan

What needs to be done: Find out if she wants to make digital scrapbooks. If so, Bethany will need to make digital files of all the images she plans to incorporate. She has a few options here: her photo organizer can do that for her (via a per-image fee or a project fee). If Bethany wants to be more do-it-yourself, she can purchase a Flip-Pal mobile scanner or a flatbed scanner and do it herself. Once she has her images scanned, she'll be ready when she wants to proceed. Having scans will preserve the images for future generations, whether she makes photo books or not. The scanned images should be backed up in multiple forms, using a flash drive stored offsite, Cloud storage, an external hard drive, or by other methods.

What to do with it: Make a small digital photo book of Christmas. She can discuss with her organizer which consumer-facing photo book provider would be best for her. Photo organizer Marci Brennan suggests some possibilities: Artifact Uprising, Blurb, ZnO, AdoramaPix, and Mixbooks. Apple recently switched printing partners, making their photobooks less expensive. Sending photos already on an iPhone direct to photobooks simplifies the process.

Where to start: Upload Christmas photos located on her smartphone to her chosen photobook provider.

When: Over the next two weeks, starting today at 2 p.m., when she watches a couple of YouTube how-to videos.

Who: Bethany will use multiple resources, including help from the photo organizer, watching how-to videos, and her own trial and error.

Bethany will:

- Search "How to Make a Photobook" on YouTube;

- Watch a few videos about how to do it;

- Set up an account with the vendor of her choice;

- Figure out how to upload her Smartphone photos to the website; and

- Set up an appointment with the photo organizer to get her started.

At that visit, the photo organizer will:

- Walk Bethany through how to create a photo book project, choosing the style, importing the uploaded photos, navigating the design tools, and saving the project;

- Assist Bethany in designing a few pages until she feels more confident; and

- Give her tips on how to select the best photos and how not to overcomplicate the process.

After the photo organizer leaves, Bethany will continue to design more pages until she has completed the small photo book. Bethany will review the project and order it. If she has any questions during this step, she will contact the photo organizer, who will talk her through it.

When Bethany receives her book in a couple of weeks, she will show it to family and evaluate the digital option versus the paper scrapbook option. She'll assess her effort for each, enjoyment or lack of enjoyment of each process, and how much she and her family like the final product of digital or paper scrapbooks. After this assessment, Bethany will decide how she would like to proceed with her memory-making goals.

Your Turn: Pause & Notice

- How do you store photos and keep memories?
- What expectations do you have for yourself?
- Why did you create those expectations?
- How reasonable are those expectations given your interest/time/ability?
- What options might you use to achieve your memory-saving goals in an easier way?
- What from Bethany's story resonated with you?
- What action steps will you take around photos and memory papers?

Take a photo of your photos and memory box things.

Discovery Questions

- Who do you need to apologize to? Why? What would you say? By saying those words, how would you feel different about yourself?

SECTION 3:

Realign Roles

CHAPTER 11

Resilience, Not Resistance

"Weeds are flowers too, once you get to know them."
Winnie the Pooh

Aging Well

We tend to think of age as our chronological ages, meaning the number of years since we were born. But that's not the whole story. Some say, "Age is just a mindset." That doesn't cover it, either. Although someone may be young in spirit, she cannot deny the biological changes of her aging body. She may try to buck social norms to "act her age" by dressing provocatively, plumping with Botox and hiding gray with hair dye, yet there is no denying that age marches on.

Getting older involves more than filling in the equation of X + Y = Z. You may have good genetics that could lead to a long life, plenty of resources to give you access to healthcare, a safe neighborhood, and the extras that money can buy, yet even that doesn't protect you from having a child die of a drug overdose—the kind of devastating life event that can reduce your lifespan. How you make decisions and think about the world, as well as how you respond to unexpected life events, greatly impacts your longevity. Your personal habits matter. Whether you are socially connected to others matters. The cumulative effect of life choices matters.

Sixty years ago, older adults in the United States had a shorter life span due to a harder physical life, less advanced healthcare, and other factors. If you think of an old person as someone who sits in a rocking chair because she is too frail to actively participate in life, you have an outdated view of aging. Life expectancy has increased by more than fifteen years in the United States. According to The U.S. Department of Health and Human Services, people born in 1934 in the U.S. had an average life expectancy of sixty years. Those born in 2014 have an average life expectancy of seventy-nine.

Societal expectations of being older have changed. Grandparents are now expected to know their grandkids, and they are often involved in their activities. Older adults are active in their communities, contributing to social movements, activism, volunteering, and creativity. While some older adults lead more passive lives, many are creating a vibrant model of aging. For example, The Villages, Florida, is a retirement community of over 115,000 people. Residents have access to golf courses, kayaking, continuing education classes, over 2,250 clubs, and many more activities.

Individuals age successfully by continuing healthy habits, lifestyles and relationships throughout their lives, including from midlife into older age. As I researched for this book, I discovered the importance of healthful behaviors in middle age. Having a slew of bad habits or disengagement in midlife will likely continue into old age, too, causing you to deteriorate faster—unless you make a conscious change. Conversely, shifting to positive habits in midlife will benefit you in later stages. Engaging in activities just for the sake of being active will not do the trick. You must engage in activities that are fulfilling or meaningful in some way. See Chapter 6 for a list of ideas of meaningful activities.

Life satisfaction depends on many things, from stress levels to how you respond to new experiences. Two primary contributors to life satisfaction are physical health and social support. When it comes to physical health, your satisfaction derives from not just the absence of illness, but from feeling good about the state of your health. Satisfaction with your social support depends not just on the number of friends you have on social media, but the quantity and quality of your interactions in everyday life. Having a home that aligns with your life requirements right now adds to your physical, emotional, and social health.

The first section of this book looked at ways to align general life changes with your day to day needs and habits. Section two focused on adjusting to changes in your home and heart related to expected life transitions like retirement and career shifts. This final section hones in on aligning your life after difficult life transitions—those losses that compound as you get older. Having a clear picture of your legacy and knowing how to be resilient are the tools you need for this part of the hero's journey.

The Developmental Tasks of Aging

What if, instead of trying to hurry the process of re-evaluating your belongings, you slowed it down to accomplish this important developmental task? According to David Solie in *How to Say It® to Seniors: Closing the Communication Gap with Our Elders*, it's not just toddlers and teens who have developmental stages to master. Older adults are tasked with discovering what he calls their "organic legacy." To find this, you sort through choices and events within your life—the good, the bad, and even things that didn't happen—to determine the values that have been most important in shaping who you are. Looking back is not something to resist; it is an essential part of the meaning-making process and the development task of the final stage of life. You must make space in your schedule and psyche for this important work.

When someone feels poorly or is recovering from a life transition, instinct tells them to delay taking action until things settle down. This approach may have worked in earlier years when there was time between losses. As a person gets older, the losses come more quickly, sometimes compounding without a quiet period during which you return to some sense of normal.

A normal reaction to feeling out of control is to seek to maintain control. When uncontrollable events happen, including being diagnosed with a chronic health condition, you must first resolve the desire to control the situation before feeling safe enough to explore the meaning of the change.

How can you create a sense of control?

- Acknowledge what is happening. First and foremost, give yourself permission to not hurry through the crisis. You are on your own timeline.

- Communicate to loved ones how they can help you. For example, if you feel like they are pressuring you to make a quick decision, explain that the best way to support you is to find ways to help you remain in control of decisions as much as possible.

- Affirm their right to their opinion and your right to yours. "I realize that you have many demands on your time and I do not want to burden you, but I have a different perspective on this. I want some time to figure it out without feeling pressure."

- Another way to say it is: "It's hard for me to convey how many losses I feel: my health is worse, my friends have moved, and some have died, new technology has changed the rules of daily life, and now you are trying to take away the home I have decades of memories in and the things that mean the most to me? I'm not trying to fight you. I don't want you to take over to fix it. I want you to help me manage it and process it."

When someone at a presentation explains how frustrated they are about their spouse or parent not cooperating, I sometimes ask them to hand me their purse or wallet. "Let me just take this and sort through it," I say. "I'll decide what makes sense for you to keep and then give it back to you." You should see the look of fear that crosses his or her face. It soon becomes obvious that they want to be the ones in charge of deciding what is and is not important to them, not a stranger and not even a loved one.

"Part of our conflict with controlling people," writes Solie, "is that we tend to fight them for the very thing they won't surrender." The longer you try to take away control from a loved one, the longer you will undermine her developmental drive to discover what is most important. This can be true for you, too, when you deny yourself permission to acknowledge that you require more processing time. In trying to speed up the process, you delay it.

Tool#1: Discovering Your Legacy

What lurks below the life transition are assumptions, past hurts, fears, unprocessed events or even processed events that need to be looked at again.

You refuse to let go of the typewriter you treasured as a child because it reminds you of hours spent hidden in your room creating poetry. It also reminds you of how your mother criticized you for having your "head in the clouds" and that you should do something more productive or risk failing in life. There's something to be sorted out here. It's not just about lacking space for a typewriter at your new home.

The adult child of someone processing their legacy can easily miss what is happening. What if your father's seemingly incongruent verbal wanderings are not signs of his mental decline? What if him rehashing the past and retelling the same stories means that he is working on the developmental task of finding his organic legacy? He is seeking to understand and accept the life that he has led. This is legacy work.

Solie distinguishes "organic legacy" from what he calls "default legacy" and "political legacy." Default legacy is what happens when someone dies, and others define the basic facts of her life or uncover information about her in the process of going through her things (such as diaries or letters). A political legacy means the person creates a way to be remembered that's motivated by doing the right thing. For example, donating money to his alma mater may or may not be a heartfelt measure, but it's an act that he feels is expected of him. An organic legacy stems from a heartfelt and complete life review. It looks at events, relationships, paths taken or not, assigning meaning and resulting in what Solie calls a "redemptive process that recontextualizes everything that may have been misinterpreted, misunderstood, or unrepaired in a person's life." An organic legacy isn't as much about having an external recognition or award as it is about being clear on what value your life brought, then sharing that with others.

A health crisis will accelerate the drive to find meaning and may even facilitate it because you are forced to step out of the fast lane. How often does someone learn she has cancer, then be taken with the urge to assess her life, write letters to her children, make amends, and record her autobiography? Becoming ill or even just noticing the permanent physical changes of aging causes people to slow down enough to reflect. In the flurry of life before, he didn't have time to contemplate; now he has many hours of contemplation.

How can you nurture your loved ones, especially your elders? Two ways, help them maintain control and listen with curiosity to their stories. What sounds like mental wandering and disjointed stories may hold clues to important memories to revisit. Can you see a values theme underlying the stories? Are there clues to an unresolved event that you can ask a follow-up question about?

If you are in the midst of delving into your own organic legacy, exchange listening hours with your friends or enlist the help of a therapist. The discovery questions at the end of each chapter are designed to help you find your organic legacy. Go back and answer these questions if you haven't already to kickstart the legacy exploration process.

Tool #2: Building Resilience

Shit happens. Yeah, I said it. I'm not going to soften it because that's what it feels like when unexpected things happen to derail our lives and who we thought we were. Part of this truth-telling is to be able to face it head-on: to name it; to cry, scream, simmer, vent, and punch pillows over it. Aging involves both growth and decline. We are challenging with finding ways to adjust along the way. The timing of decline—whether physical, mental or emotional—is not a pre-determined certainty. How you react matters.

Losses may pile up as the years pass. A health crisis, the death of loved ones, having your lifelong friend move, and experiencing a financial loss are all examples of significant events that jar you out of what you are used to, sending you scrambling to adjust. Transition theorist Peter Jarvis called this experience "disjunctures." Jarvis believed that "even mis-educative experiences may be regarded as learning experiences." Most importantly, the meaning you give to the experiences determines how you will go through the transition. Another way to say it is that your perspective—the story you tell yourself—about what happened is perhaps even more important than the event itself.

Looking from a New Perspective

Think of a difficult time of your life. What happened? Do you still feel angry or hurt from that time or did it dissipate after a while? In any story, the hero doesn't have merely one thing happen to him before his life is over. Look at the character Harry Potter. His parents were killed, he was sent to live in a home where they made him sleep in a closet, and he did not learn important details about himself until age eleven when he went to school at Hogwarts. In every book in the Harry Potter series, his life is threatened by the worst of the worst. Someone who has one thing after another happen to him, especially as a young child, could consider himself as Victim Number One, the person who will always be bullied, locked away, and treated poorly. While Harry questions the events and struggles with the unique role that he has been given, he perseveres, and he learns resilience. I realize Harry is a fictional character. But the hero's journey that he embodies gives us an empowering perspective. How can we overcome the unexpected and significant losses that we encounter? Let's explore this.

Think again of that difficult time in your life that I asked you to bring to mind in the last paragraph. Let's say you were fired from a job. You hated that job because no matter what you did, you could not please the boss. Every day you woke up with a pit in your stomach because you didn't want to spend the next eight hours walking on eggshells and feeling like your boss would reprimand you for something you were unable to anticipate. Then you got fired. It was embarrassing to carry your box of belongings from your desk past all the people in your department. You felt ashamed to tell your wife what happened, but you couldn't avoid that. It took a few weeks before you found another position. It paid a little less, and you loved the new boss and co-workers. You knew the expectations and worked hard to prove yourself. After six months you were at the previous job's salary, and within a year, you got a promotion with a raise.

My questions are: Do you mourn the injustice of how you were fired and experienced intense, though temporary, negative emotions? Or do you celebrate that getting fired pushed you to get a job with clear expectations, a great work environment, and opportunities to advance? What story are you telling yourself? When you are used to telling yourself a story for a long time about how you were wronged, it can be a challenge to tell a new story. There's an emotional payoff for you to hang on to the story of yourself as a victim.

It's time to ask the tough question: "What am I getting out of continuing to tell this story?" To help you get practice telling a new story, let's look at some examples:

Roadside Assistance

Betsy's car broke down one day on the way home from work. She had just begun her professional life and didn't have extra money to pay for repairs, which is why she drove a clunker car. The breakdown happened during a spring rainstorm, right after sunset, so it was hard to see. Shortly after the car broke down, a truck pulled over, and a man about her age emerged. Betsy wondered if she was going to get murdered on top of having a car emergency. Turns out that Larry, the guy who stopped to help, was a mechanic who lived a couple blocks from her apartment building. Betsy reminded Larry of his sister who had just moved to another city and who had been on his mind all day. Larry got a buddy to tow her car to his shop, then Larry gave her a ride home. Larry and Betsy enjoyed each other's company so much during this chance encounter that they set up a date to see each other again.

What's the story here?

- ❑ Betsy had the rotten luck of having her car break down in a storm;
- ❑ The kindness of a stranger led to something better;
- ❑ Crappy things happen to people who can't afford it; or
- ❑ People are more often kind than cruel.

Treatment Buddy

Adam was just diagnosed with testicular cancer. Doctors caught it early, and the surgery showed that the tumor was malignant. He needed to undergo chemotherapy treatments after having his testes removed. At the same time, Adam's Dad began treatments for lung cancer. Although the two had been living in the same community, Adam and his father didn't spend much time together outside of a few holidays throughout the year. His dad's diagnosis scared Adam. He felt like he didn't know his father very well due to all the hours his Dad had worked while Adam was growing up. Adam wasn't sure how to approach his Dad after the lung cancer was diagnosed.

A cancer care clinic doctor who heard about the father-son cancer story mentioned that it was possible for them to schedule treatments at the same times as long as white blood cell counts stayed on track for each. They were able to be treatment buddies a couple of times, and it felt like making a new friend. The cancer diagnoses leveled the playing field for them to get to know each other in a new way. It was hard for Adam to see his father looking so thin and pale, but Adam knew he also looked like hell. He felt like hell, too. He never would have chosen cancer to bring him and his Dad together. But there they were, sitting side by side in identical tan vinyl chairs, alternating stories, jokes, companionable silence, and shedding a few tears, too.

What's the story here?

- ❏ Family gets inundated with not one, but two cancer cases;
- ❏ Adam gets close to his father in an unexpected way;
- ❏ Cancer sucks; or

❏   Cancer sucks, but something valuable is gained.

More than Making Lemonade

There's nothing more annoying than when something terrible happens to you, and someone tells you to look on the bright side. It feels mighty dismissive as if they just want you to shut up about your difficulty, so they don't have to deal with it. That's not what I am asking you to do. It feels awful when bad things happen. If life has handed you lemons, you need a little time to scrunch up your face about how sour they are. In fact, it's essential that you spend time reacting to the sucky-ness of it to register the reality of what is happening. After a little while, though, scrunching your face at the sourness doesn't serve a purpose. At that point, your figurative taste buds are burned out, causing you to only register more of the same.

Making lemonade out of lemons is another way of acknowledging that a crappy thing happened, but that you are going to be the one who decides how to interpret the outcome. For myself, I love the question, "What is this here to teach me?" If my instinctive reaction to the question is anger, I know I'm asking too soon. Once I am past the initial shock of the unwelcome event, asking this question always reframes my perspective. I mean, if I can learn something from the crappy thing that happened, then it has a purpose; it's not just a crappy thing. Many times, my willingness to investigate that purpose has completely shifted my life experience from one of victimhood to one of power. This isn't just mumbo-jumbo bullshit. I mean it.

In 2015, my eighth-grade daughter had to be hospitalized in an adolescent behavior-health unit (the current word for psych ward). She was in crisis. It felt more intense than adolescent hormonal angst, even in this tricky time of social media pressure. We were in new and high stakes territory. It's hard to convey what it feels like to visit your teen in a double-door locked unit where patients cannot have shoes with laces due to the suicide risk. Her eyes pled "get me out of here," and my heart plummeted into my nauseated stomach. *Am I doing the right thing? Will we figure this out? What's going to happen in the future? What's going to happen tomorrow? How do I explain this to school and family and friends?*

Little by little, we did figure it out. It took two more hospitalizations, lots of education on my part, and the efforts of an effective team that included a psychiatrist we trusted, a therapist who was a good match for her, and a pediatrician who actually gave me her cell phone number. My daughter was diagnosed with bipolar depression. After a few months, she found the right combination of medicines to stabilize her moods. When her moods stabilized, she began the work of dialectical behavioral therapy interventions to cultivate habits that support her well-being. Some of these habits included taking her medication as prescribed, getting enough sleep, and eating healthy foods. She also learned strategies to manage turbulent teen issues and ones specific to her situation. I am so proud of her perseverance. She amazes me.

Talk about an awful situation! I felt like I was responsible for whether my kid would live or die. My vigilance was constant. *How was her mood? Was she truthful? Should I search her room? Was I to blame?* I didn't realize until later how co-dependent my own behavior was, and how much personal reflection I needed to do to support her (and myself) effectively. I researched the concept of co-dependence by watching videos and reading books. I asked myself difficult questions like "Was I trying to save her from herself?" and "Is my reaction sending her a message that she is incapable of stability without me?" I had to let go of several unhelpful stories, such as "This shouldn't be happening to us" and "Only I can save her."

Because I was able to alter my perspective, I could interpret the story of her health crisis in an empowering way and make that proverbial lemonade. My perspective shifted because of the question, "What is this here to teach me?" I learned that the answer was actually mostly about me. (In the end, we can only change our own behavior anyway.) I needed to learn about healthy boundaries in a relationship that literally was life or death.

There was nothing easy about this personal situation. In addition to learning about healthy boundaries, I have learned an essential truth: we only have today. My daughter's stability may change tomorrow or next month or next year. I'm not going to waste my time and energy worrying about it. The idea that I could control the future was a lie all along. I am grateful for today. I am amazed at how she has stepped into her wellness. I am able to have healthy boundaries and not ones that make me more responsible for others than they are for themselves.

While I would not have asked for this "growth opportunity," I am so, so grateful that it happened when it did and that we created a team to navigate it. I have emerged from the initial three years of the crisis a much healthier and mindful person. The situation has shown me that my interpretation of what happens to me makes all the difference. Finding positive aspects in a difficult time form the building blocks of both who I am and who I am becoming.

Not Resistance, But Resilience

When you cannot accept that what is happening *is* happening you are resisting, and all your energy is wrapped up in fighting the situation. Remember at the beginning of the book when I said the truth will set you free? Until you can acknowledge the truth of a situation's existence, you will stay stuck. Articulating how you persisted in the face of difficulty speaks to your resilience. You continued living even when your grief was so intense that you put the gallon of milk into a kitchen cabinet instead of the fridge. You found a way to get out of bed to attend the support group so you would not feel alone in your journey. These actions don't take away the loss. They prove you are stronger than you realized and that you can find your way, even when that way looks different than you ever imagined.

The stories in the following chapters dig into some major life transitions. While there are aspects that involve getting your house in order, the focus is more on seeing the growth opportunity and beginning the process of choosing a new perspective, reconnecting to your core values, and deepening your resilience.

Discovery Questions

- What are some signs that you feel overwhelmed?
- Tell me about a time when you had a big project. How did you handle it? Did you work alone or with others? What helped the process go smoothly? What made it worse?

CHAPTER 12

Keeper of the Legacy

"We can travel a long way in life and do many things, but our deepest happiness is not born from accumulating new experiences. It is born from letting go of what is unnecessary, and knowing ourselves to be always at home."
Sharon Salzberg

Jennifer's Story

Jennifer's Mom and Dad died within six months of each other in 2010. This difficult time was made more challenging because her parents had lived in the same home for forty-five years. Her sister, Michelle, traveled in from out of state to help work through the tidy, but a full four-bedroom family home. Michelle immediately suggested a dumpster and joked about giving the house the "match treatment." Jennifer, who lived in the same community as her parents and often helped them, was also overwhelmed by such a large job, yet she couldn't believe Michelle's lack of respect for their parents' things. "So typical of Michelle," she thought, "only thinking of herself."

Throughout the week, they went through closet after closet and drawer after drawer until Jennifer's brain felt like silly putty and her stomach felt queasy. Jennifer was often reminded that they had to move faster because Michelle had a limited number of vacation days. They held off dealing with special items by placing them in one bedroom and then turned the rest over to an estate sale company. Michelle felt guilty about letting some items go into the sale, and also was relieved. About sixty percent of the items sold. Before the haul away crew took the rest for donation, Jennifer found herself filling boxes of things that didn't sell and several large pieces of furniture. "These things are too special to be donated," she thought. "I'll store them in my garage until I can find a good home for them."

Over the next two years, every time Jennifer tried to sort through the boxes, she only got half a box in before it became too much. "I need a little more time," she assessed. "They haven't been gone very long."

Jennifer's husband, Dan, was patient at first. He tolerated being unable to get to his tools and having their cars parked outside for two winters. When Jennifer went to visit her sister, Dan decided to move everything to the basement. Dan, who believed he was helpful, couldn't wait to surprise her.

However, he was the one to be surprised when Jennifer broke down in tears. "I'm doing my best! I've tried to go through their stuff, and the first time I go away, you sneak it all down to the basement. I can see a clean garage is more important than my feelings!"

After a while, Jennifer and Dan made up. Jennifer was glad to not have to defrost her car windows and constantly be reminded of the big project when she passed it every day. More years passed. Each January, she told herself that this was the year to get the basement cleaned out. Each spring she considered taking time off work to really dig into the boxes, but something always came up. "Maybe in the fall," she thought.

Jennifer and Dan used to host parties. Now they couldn't due to the chance that someone would see the basement. Not having parties was easier than going through her parent's belongings.

When Dan's dad had a stroke, his parents decided to move to a continuous care retirement community. Since Jennifer had already been through this process, she led the way to downsize Dan's parents' household. All of a sudden, their garage filled up again. Jennifer and Dan fought every day. Suddenly, it wasn't the fate of the objects in the balance; it was the fate of their marriage. Something had to change.

Pause & Notice

- What problems does Jennifer see?
- What problems do others see?
- What factors may be making it hard for Jennifer to make decisions?
- What kinds of negative labels do you imagine Jennifer puts upon herself?
- What role has Jennifer taken on in the family?
- What advice would you give Jennifer?

Jennifer's Tipping Point

PAIN OF REMAINING THE SAME	PAIN OF CHANGING	BENEFITS OF CHANGING
Feeling the burden of the big project	Having to make tough decisions	Not fighting with her husband
Having the clutter threaten their marriage	Feeling like she is throwing away her parents' lives	Being able to use her basement
Not being able to use their basement	Feeling like she is letting down her family	Not having the burden of the

		unfinished projects
Not having friends over due to embarrassment	Spending time to get the big projects done	Being able to have friends over
Having the garage full again		Storing her cars in the garage
Parking outside		Finding a way to feel like she has done her job as a daughter
		Learning how to make tough decisions

Visualize Success

- Success for Jennifer and Dan would look like working together to empty their garage and basement so that each space functions as intended.

- Success would feel like being relieved of the burden of the stuff and the expectations connected to the stuff. Jennifer would honor her parents' memories but not sacrifice her own well-being and relationship.

Project Action Plan Pre-Work

Before working together, they created a list of questions that would help them to make decisions:

- Is this in the top 10 list of things that I would keep from my parents?
- Will keeping this make my house more crowded?
- Am I willing to get rid of something of similar size to make space for this?
- If this was in a store, would I buy it?
- How long will it take to use this up?

Jennifer and Dan's Project Action Plan

What needs to be done: Both the garage and basement need to be reduced by eighty percent.

What to do with it: Donate or sell what isn't kept.

Where to start: Since both spaces were big projects, the way to decide the starting spot depends upon what feels most doable for Jennifer. It may be that going through the garage items would be less daunting because Dan's family's belongings have less significance to her. If so, she should start there and build her decision-making muscles. Another advantage of clearing the garage would be to park the cars there again. A clear garage would build momentum because they see it every day.

When: Friday and Saturday, starting at 9 a.m. each day.

Who: Jennifer, Dan, and a professional organizer.

Dan will:

- Make a list of priority items he wants to keep of his parents' things;
- Decide which he will keep of duplicates related to tools, gardening, and the other household areas he manages.

Jennifer will:

- Make a list of priority items she wants to keep of Dan's parents' things;
- For household items, decide if there is space to store consumables like paper plates, toiletries, etc., and weigh how long it may take to use them against having to store them; and

- Decide which she will keep of duplicates related to the kitchen, furniture, décor, and other household areas she manages.

The Organizer will:
- Help keep Jennifer and Dan moving through the items;
- Remind them of their goal to have a garage they can park in; and
- Remind them of their desire to have a house that isn't overstuffed.

Even though the things were from Dan's parents, very few of them were sentimental to him. Most of the items were extra household belongings and clothing, with a few furniture pieces.

When Zombies Attack

Redefine Roles

Sometimes we assume roles that we didn't know we were taking on. In this case, Jennifer has taken on the role of being the "keeper of the legacy." No one explicitly gave her this assignment. As the daughter who lived near her parents, she naturally became the caregiver of them, and, by extension, their things.

When her caregiver role converged with how she handled her parent's things, it placed her in a bind of feeling like she was discarding her parents by getting rid of things. She knew this was a non-rational association, but she felt helpless to do things differently, especially when it came to furniture pieces that her parents inherited from their parents. Articulating the unstated expectations of "keeper of the legacy" may help her break free. Jennifer could consider these questions.

1) What assumptions has she been making about what she *should* do with these inherited items?

2) How would her parents react if they knew she donated inherited items?

3) Would her parents prefer her to keep the inherited items if it means that she cannot use rooms in her home, she is arguing with her husband because of it, and she is disconnected from having friends over?

4) In what ways was she a good daughter to her parents?

5) Does she want the role of keeping *all* of the inherited items?

6) What would she want her own kids to experience when they are in her stage of life?

7) What other ways can she honor her parents, and also, her own needs?

Ideas to honor a loved one

An audience member at one of my presentations found herself in this situation. Her voice had a desperate edge as she shared the problem. "My mom insisted that take my grandmother's buffet. I already have one of my own, plus one from my husband's parents. We do not have room for three buffets. What can I do?"

She hadn't realized that she had been appointed as "keeper of the legacy." After she became conscious about the role, she said it was not one she wanted. We talked about alternatives. Of the three buffets, the one from her grandmother was the one she wanted to get rid of.

"What did your grandmother enjoy doing?" I asked.

"She was a big bowler. Also, she loved the St. Louis Cardinals."

"What if you could honor your grandmother in a different way, a way that would not take space from your young family, and that would celebrate who she was in a way that helps your kids remember her?"

Her shoulders relaxed and she looked at me intently. I could tell she was relieved that she could do something besides keep the large furniture piece. She looked curious about what I might suggest.

"What if you sell the buffet and use the money to go bowling with your family?" I asked. "Tell them stories about your memories of her and how much she loved to bowl. The whole night will be a celebration of her, doing something she loved. Doesn't that honor her more than feeling annoyed to keep something that you don't have room for and don't like?"

She smiled. "That sounds fun, but what about my mom? Won't she be angry that I didn't keep it?"

"I'm guessing your mom doesn't realize she has made herself and you 'keeper of the legacy' or that she has an alternative. You may find that sharing this with her will give her permission to make her own choices, too."

She nodded, but her lips were pursed and she let out a big sigh. I could tell she thought I had no idea what her mother could be like.

"Tell her your plan to honor her mother, and say she can have the buffet at her house if she wants it. I'm guessing she doesn't have room, which means she won't get to continue using your house as her free storage unit or as a way to avoid making a decision."

She raised her eyebrows. Clearly, she hadn't considered that she was letting her house be someone's free storage unit or that her mom was avoiding her own guilty feelings.

"Invite her to the bowling party," I continued, "and stick to your plan. *You* get to decide what you keep in your house. Not anyone else."

She sat a little straighter after hearing that. I could sense her resolve building.

You are the Boss of Your House

I often affirm a person's right to choose what does or does not belong in his or her home. It sometimes feels like they've been waiting for someone to give them that permission. Let me give you that permission, too. You are the boss of what is in your house. You are the gatekeeper blocking what comes in and the landlord who evicts what's not working out.

If you don't stand up for your interests, then who will? Your job as boss of your house is to create a home environment that, first and foremost, accounts for the requirements of the people who live there. Imagine having a house that only has what you use and love. Think of how empowered you would be to move through each day without the guilt, burden, chaos, and stress the extra stuff causes you.

You get to decide. Not anyone outside of your home. If anyone gives you guff about it, just say Kate, the organizer, says that's how you are supposed to do it.

Let me tell you about another epidemic among those in the "sandwich generation" (those who are caring for their aging parents and their own children). I call this epidemic "I thought you could use this" syndrome. This is when your loved ones, who have not learned the art of letting go, unload their stuff onto you by the box load. You may think that you are obligated to keep the stuff because, in the past, they have only given you things that were desirable gifts. These boxes are different. They contain things like half a box of yellow stir sticks, Thanksgiving-themed paper plates from 1983, a set of crystal brandy snifters, your school photos, a macaroni necklace you made in 2nd grade, a candy dish they got in Holland, a poncho that smells of stale rubber, a stack of partially used notebooks, a Hard Rock café Hurricane glass, and other junk. These boxes put the miss in miscellaneous.

Who am I to say you won't use these things? Maybe you are planning a retro Thanksgiving cocktail party. My point here is, don't assume you have to keep them forever just because they were given to you by someone you love. That loving person may unknowingly be using you as her way to avoid the feelings that come from throwing away a perfectly good half box of yellow stir sticks purchased for the company party of 1972. Let me say loud and clear that *you* get to decide.

Let's consider what might transpire if you decide not to keep this mélange of assorted items.

Scenario 1: Your loved ones don't ask about the items later and blissfully continue to give you things as they clear out their home. No issues here, except you have become their default junk transport system. My advice is to continue to take the boxes, and then do what you like with them. You can also choose to take a stand, but realize that will force your loved ones to begin to confront their awful feelings, which, if they don't get help to do so, will result in the entire downsizing process coming to a halt.

Scenario 2: Your loved ones begin to suspect you are throwing away their precious potpourri of possessions. At your next visit, as they hand you the next box, they say, "Well, I don't know if I should give this to you. You are probably just going to throw it away." Then they will sigh deeply and give it to you anyway. You may just smile and take the boxes, or you can say, "An expert named Kate said you should never give things with strings attached about what to do with them." Then carry the box to your car. If you are feeling really saucy, you can say, "What's the alternative to giving it to me?"

Scenario 3: Your loved ones get angry that you are not keeping the items or using up the Thanksgiving-themed paper plates. If this is the case, refuse to take any more boxes. Not only do you get to be in charge of what you keep in your house, but you also get to be in charge of your emotions. And that box is filled with stuff, and a weighty scoop of guilt and obligation. No thanks.

If you are the giver of these boxes, choose your scenario or man up and get help to learn how to let go. I mean that in the most loving way possible.

How to Pick Your Top Ten Inherited Items

- Is this meaningful to my loved one and to me?

- Is this just meaningful to my loved one?

- Do I have space for this?

- Is there another way to remember it?

- What if I didn't have it?

- Would I try to save it in an emergency?

- If I keep this, will it just sit in a box in the attic or will I display it/enjoy it?

- Narrow it further: Which of these things best represents my loved one and/or what I want to remember?

Jennifer's Habit Action Plan

What needs to be done: Improve her skill of deciding what to keep or not.

What to do with it: Hone in on what she wants and honor that.

Where to start: In the basement with her parents' things.

When: Monday at 9 a.m.

Who: Jennifer and the same professional organizer.

Jennifer will:

- Create an area for things in her Top Ten List of Inherited Items to Keep;

- Practice the process of asking herself these key questions:

  o Do I love this the most?

  o Do I have room for this?

  o Could I live without it?

- Use the gratitude technique from Chapter 7 to let go of objects that served her parents and that she doesn't want to keep;

- Set a timer to go off every thirty minutes to remind her to notice her energy levels, whether she needs food, water, or a short break, and to celebrate her progress; and
- Schedule as many additional sessions with the support of the organizer as it takes to complete the basement and make the final cuts until she has her Top Ten (or whatever number she decides makes sense).

The Organizer will:

- Help create an open space as a staging area, with an area near the stairs for items to be donated, sturdy bags for trash, and a table on which to place the possible Top Ten grouping;
- Give Jennifer support as she practices the decision questions and the gratitude technique;
- Keep Jennifer focused on one box at a time, possibly even handing her one thing at a time as she decides;
- Reinforce Jennifer's confidence as she learns to trust her instincts and honor what she wants;
- Help Jennifer see how much she is accomplishing both in physical sorting and in improving her decision-making skills; and
- Continue to work through the basement boxes with Jennifer until it is complete and she has chosen her Top Ten.

Your Turn: Pause & Notice

- Have you filled your space with items you've inherited or that you haven't felt you could decide upon?

- What options might you use to honor a loved one rather assume the role of "keeper of the legacy"?
- What from Jennifer's story resonated with you?
- What action steps will you take around inherited items?

Take a photo of inherited items to be sorted.

Discovery Questions

- What's the best trip you ever took?
- Who were you with?
- What did you see?
- What made this trip better than others?
- What did you realize about yourself from going there?

CHAPTER 13

If Only I Hadn't Waited!

"Mindfulness is the aware, balanced acceptance of the present experience. It isn't more complicated than that. It is opening to or receiving the present moment, pleasant or unpleasant, just as it is, without either clinging to it or rejecting it."
Sylvia Boorstein

Danielle's Story

Danielle didn't get her formal diagnosis of ADHD until she was fifty-three. It was something she suspected all along, joked about having, but felt shocked to officially have. Suddenly it all made sense: always being late, the messy apartment, starting project after project without finishing, forgetting meetings with friends, fielding calls from collection agencies, and on and on.

Her mother's explained Danielle's missing school work by saying her daughter was lazy. Her bosses over the years gave her performance reviews with phrases like, "bright, but inconsistent" and "has difficulty meeting deadlines and arriving on time." Danielle's solution was to try harder.

Her current supervisor, Nancy, was the one who encouraged her to get tested for ADHD. Two of Nancy's children had Attention Deficit/Hyperactivity Disorder, as well as Nancy herself. About ten years earlier, Danielle's nephew had been diagnosed with it.

Her sister also urged her to see a psychologist and get tested. "I can pay attention just fine—when I want to," Danielle explained. "Besides, I'm not bouncing off the walls. I'm just a procrastinator." That procrastination caused her to lose three jobs in fifteen years and possibly even her marriage.

In addition to seeing a psychologist twice a month, Danielle tried different medications. The process took longer than she expected. When she finally got the right medication, she couldn't believe the difference! She completed a major project as well as a few small ones without waiting to start until the night before or asking for an extension.

At home, Danielle's laundry wasn't getting moldy in the washer, even though she still lived out of her laundry basket and had entirely too many clothes. Cleaning up her dishes didn't feel so hard. Before the diagnosis, she would have grabbed a take-out dinner and landed on the sofa watching Netflix. Most of the time, the garbage piled up on the coffee table and floor until she did a marathon cleaning session.

Danielle couldn't figure out why she felt so sad. Part of her wondered what would have happened if she had known about having ADHD ten years earlier. Even though things were a little better, she felt like such a failure. Her house was a jumbled-up mess and she didn't know where to start or even how to do it.

Pause & Notice

- What problems does Danielle see?
- What problems do others see?
- How did Danielle explain her behavior in the past?
- Why would Danielle have mixed feelings about finally getting answers about her life struggles?

- What resources or support does Danielle already have?

- What stands in the way of Danielle doing things differently?

- What advice would you give Danielle?

Danielle's Tipping Point (for adjusting her home post-diagnosis)

PAIN OF REMAINING THE SAME	PAIN OF CHANGING	BENEFITS OF CHANGING
Living in a mess	Asking for help from yet another person	Feeling calmer when she is at home
Feeling like a failure	Taking the time to sort through the backlog	Being able to find clean clothes
Being overwhelmed by the backlog of stuff	Having to learn new skills	Having an organizing system that she can maintain easier
Difficulty finding clothes	Worrying that she will continue to fail	Pride in learning to keep up her space
Still running late		Being late less frequently
		Better sleep
		Having people over

Visualize Success

- Success would look like something Danielle cannot even imagine to be possible for her, since she had never experienced it. Distinguishing between her unattainable ideal of being organized versus being "good enough" would be important to having a functional home.
- Success for Danielle meant household tasks would not feel so hard.

Danielle's Project Action Plan

What needs to be done: Organize Danielle's apartment and create manageable systems that account for her ADHD tendencies.

What to do with it: Eliminate what she doesn't use and streamline what she is keeping.

Where to start: Her bedroom.

When: Saturday at 1:30 p.m.

Who: A professional organizer who specializes in ADHD. It's very important for Danielle to choose an organizer who is an ADHD expert because traditional organizing methods are often a mismatch for someone with ADHD. An organizer who doesn't understand ADHD may be unable to support Danielle in the ways she needs to be supported. Danielle searched online for "professional organizer ADHD + [her city]" and talked with three organizers, choosing the one that seemed like the best fit.

Danielle will:
- Do as much laundry as she can before the appointment;
- Have bags or boxes to fill with donations;

- Make decisions on the clothes and shoes that are being presorted into categories by the organizer: keep, donate, toss, try on;
- Let the organizer know of any types of things that can be tossed (e.g., old newspapers, store bags, empty take-out containers);
- Talk through her laundry process, including what has worked and not worked in the past, her expectations, both the ideal version and the simplest version;
- Talk through her morning routine for getting ready, including what has worked and not worked in the past, her expectations, both the ideal versions and the simplest version;
- Help tidy up what is kept and take out the trash and donations;
- Set up another organizing appointment to work on things found in the bedroom that belong elsewhere; and
- Get clear on what system she will try for laundry and for her morning routine.

The ADHD Specialist Organizer will:

- Ask Danielle to create guidelines on what she will keep (see below) and post the list temporarily on the wall of the bedroom;
- Presort the clothes into categories so Danielle can make decisions within a grouping;
- Be attuned to when Danielle's energy is getting low and suggest a break;

- Group other things that are scattered around the bedroom to sort later: important papers and money, less important papers, personal care items, kitchen items, books/magazines, and any other like items;

- Listen carefully to Danielle's explanation of her laundry process and morning routine, ask follow-up questions and begin setting up a system based on what has already worked and what might be the simplest approach. There will be follow-up and tweaking after Danielle experiments with the system;

- Tidy up what is being kept;

- Remove the trash and take donations for drop-off;

- Create a plan for the next visit; and

- Establish when she will contact Danielle next to see how the systems are going.

Danielle's List of Clothes to Keep

- Fits her now;

- Looks good on her and makes her feel confident;

- Feels good when she wears it (is not itchy);

- No holes; and

- Doesn't have too many duplicates of the same thing, in which case she will pick her favorites.

When Zombies Attack

ADHD is a Brain-Based Condition

Attention Deficit/Hyperactivity Disorder is a real condition that negatively impacts people's lives significantly. Researcher Russell Barkley, speaking at the 2018 CHADD conference, said that ADHD can shorten people's lives by eleven to thirteen years. It is a public health crisis more prevalent than obesity and substance abuse. ADHD affects between four and twelve percent of school-aged children and is present in an estimated four to five percent of adults. ADHD is now known to be a disorder that persists into adulthood, causing difficulty in daily social, occupational, and relational functioning. Or, as one of my clients told me, "My ADHD affects every part of every day, all of the time."

There are three core symptoms of ADHD: inattention, hyperactivity, and impulsivity. In adults, inattention means losing things, having trouble paying attention when others speak, making careless mistakes, difficulty getting started on tasks—particularly ones which are routine—and keeping attention on a task. Hyperactivity shows up as fidgeting and constant motion, excessive talking, and can shift in adulthood from the outward restlessness to a mind that always races. Impulsive behavior means taking action without pausing, which can cause all sorts of issues with finances, health, relationships, and work success. Examples include constantly interrupting your boss, co-workers, and spouse, choosing what to do in the moment rather than by priority, spending money on new and exciting things, and automatic eating. Without the pause created by strong executive functions, these symptoms cause serious issues.

While most people exhibit some of these behaviors some of the time, people with ADHD experience symptoms to such an extent that it impairs two or more areas of their lives. Because ADHD is often misunderstood, I'd like to briefly explain how it is brain-based. The frontal lobe—specifically the pre-frontal cortex, located just behind your forehead—acts as the "boss" of the brain, managing tasks collectively known as "executive functions." Executive functions include paying attention to tasks, focusing and sustaining concentration, making good decisions, planning ahead, learning, and remembering what we have learned. Emotions such as anger, frustration, and irritability are related to activity in the pre-frontal cortex as well.

Hyperactivity, talking out of turn, and sudden anger or frustration—often aspects of ADHD—should be stopped by the inhibitory mechanisms of the cortex. When the brain isn't properly inhibited, these behaviors occur. According to the ADHD Information Library, the limbic system lies deeper in the brain and acts as our emotional center. An over-active limbic system can result in wide mood swings or outbursts of temper. In contrast, a normally functioning limbic system produces smooth emotional changes, consistent energy levels, sleep patterns, and better stress tolerance.

Researchers have been studying ADHD for decades, and there is much to discover about it. Clinical Psychologist Thomas Brown explains that ADHD is "essentially a chemical problem, specifically in the chemical system that supports rapid and efficient communication in the brain's management system." The human brain holds about 100 billion neurons, tiny cells that send information to other cells. Neurons connect with other neurons through the axon terminal at junctions called synapses. Key to the synaptic process is the effective release and slowed reuptake of the transmitter chemicals dopamine and norepinephrine—two of the chemicals critical to executive functioning. In other words, the part of the brain that manages tasks that we need to be organized, in control, and have persistent attention is not producing the chemicals needed to make executive functions work. Some ADHD medicines *stimulate* these chemical synapses to function properly.

There may be days when someone with ADHD feels clear-headed, and they are able to produce. They don't know why this happened. It feels good to have a working brain. When others notice the better functioning, they conclude that the person with ADHD is someone who can do what is expected, but who is intentionally not doing it, perhaps out of laziness or stubbornness. The person's good day is held against them, when the brain is back to not working the next day. Not being able to control productivity leads to that person feeling like a failure.

The only consistency with untreated or undertreated ADHD is inconsistency. That inconsistency results from a brain-based condition of chemical synapses that are not functioning properly. Medicine is certainly not the only treatment; however, it's an essential treatment for many people. I'll get to additional treatment modes below. There is so much more to know about ADHD and Executive Functioning. Because many people with ADHD aren't big readers, a wonderful way to increase ADHD knowledge is through www.HowToADHD.com. Jessica McCabe, its founder, and host, has created hundreds of engaging and educational videos.

Now that you have learned this much, do you have a different perspective on Danielle's story? Your own? Danielle, like many women who are diagnosed with ADHD in mid-life, not only has to contend with understanding her diagnosis, to figure out the right medication and right amount of medication, and to develop new strategies, but she has a layer of negative self-talk that is deeply embedded. Up until now, her only explanation for her uneven performance was that she shouldn't be so lazy and to try harder. As she learns more about how ADHD is based in the brain, she can begin to understand her brain requires treatment just as a person with diabetes needs insulin. The process of understanding this and adjusting to it will take time.

Help on the Journey

The book, *Journeys Through ADDulthood,* by Sari Solden blazed a trail for understanding the issues experienced by people, particularly women, diagnosed with ADHD in adulthood. Solden, a psychotherapist who also has ADHD, created a conversation around what it was like to learn you have ADHD later in life, and how that created an identity crisis around what the diagnosis meant about your past, present, and future.

Solden has created a treatment model called M.E.S.S.T., which stands for Medication, Education, Support, Strategies, and Therapy. I love this acronym because it presents a full picture of managing ADHD. It's not only medicine or only strategies. Solden emphasizes how implementing the M.E.S.S.T model happens in stages. It starts by getting diagnosed, which can feel like such a relief. Really, so much happens after diagnosis. These steps include learning about your ADHD, finding the right medicine and the right amount of medicine, enlisting allies like therapists, CHADD (Children and Adults with ADHD) peer support groups, ADHD coaches, professional organizers, housecleaners, financial planners, and using strategies involving smartphone apps, calendars, timers, and simple systems that can be maintained.

Tuning in to strengths

I have never known anyone who is compelled to change because of how terrible they have made themselves feel. The path to success is not paved with stones made from guilt and shame. And even worse, trying to motivate yourself by putting yourself down only makes your feet sink further into the quicksand of being stuck.

The alternative to negative reinforcement involves building upon your strengths. Shifting from the habit of putting yourself down to acknowledging what you do well can be surprisingly difficult. It's a little like eating dessert before dinner or playing before your chores are finished. Deeply ingrained in the American psyche is the work first, play second mindset. When it comes to ADHD, this mindset is especially unhelpful because tedious tasks never get completely done.

Let's take a different approach by looking at your strengths. Consider whether your strengths include inventiveness, flexibility, resourcefulness, or exuberance. Perhaps you excel at the ability to connect with anyone, having a great sense of humor, and a wide set of interests. Knowing your strengths allows you to use those attributes to design your strategies instead of idealizing the elusive ways you "should" be doing things. Usually the "should" version is associated with traditional organizing methods, which I will discuss shortly. The concept to take in here is to stop aligning yourself with complex strategies. Surely you have tried and failed to do things the "should" way. These include buying a new book, tool, piece of equipment, or time management system, thinking "willpower" will help you do something consistently every day. The next part of ineffective, "should" systems are berating yourself to spark getting to action, or doing a marathon cleaning session, which results in exhausting you so much that the progress reverts to a mess.

Unconventional organizing techniques

The secret to create manageable systems with ADHD is to reduce the number of belongings you manage and to create a system with few steps. Let's look at some examples of unconventional organizing techniques compared to the techniques that are typically put forward.

Managing Clothing

The traditional method for clothing is hanging clean clothes in a closet or storing them in a drawer. Dirty clothes are sorted by color and type to be washed, dried, then hung up or folded, and put away. An unconventional method might bypass drawers and use open bins or even using a laundry basket to hold clean clothes. Instead of hanging clothes in a closet, an unconventional method involves using hooks to hang up clothes that will be worn again. An unconventional laundry process might skip the sorting process and wash everything in cold with a Shout Color Catcher, dry them and put them "away" in the open bins.

Managing Paper

Traditionally, paper gets sorted and filed in a file drawer. A more ADHD-friendly way of managing paper simplifies the process. Get as many accounts as possible to be paperless online with automatic deduction. Get off catalog lists at www.catalogchoice.org. Be aware that once you order from a catalog again, they will be delivered again, plus all the other catalogs that company shares your mailing information with. Make a few rules for yourself. When you get the mail, immediately recycle the junk mail. Be creative! Label your garbage can or recycling bin as "the junk mail monster" that you need to feed. Don't tell yourself you will read an interesting article later because you probably won't.

If a piece of mail demands an action, immediately write that action on the envelope. When an action will only take a couple of minutes, do it right away. Mail that requires a longer timeframe should be slotted into a specific time and placed in a routine place like a small basket on the kitchen counter. Do not use a big basket or bin because you want to encourage getting the tasks done sooner. Here's a tip: the size of the container provides a visual cue for when to clear it out. A big container will take a long time to fill, while a small container gets full fast. Choose something that is no taller than an inch.

Next, establish a routine for performing those actions. I've noticed that people follow through better when they are already up and moving. Make the ten minutes after you clear your dish at dinner be the time you complete some actions. Because you have already identified what should be done, you can batch your actions. For example, pay a few bills or make a few calls. Set an alarm on your phone for that time of day as an external reminder, or make a sign with colorful paper that temporarily hangs above the sink until you incorporate the new habit. You may need to make a new sign in a couple of weeks and hang it another place. People with ADHD thrive on novelty. After a while, the reminder stops working and that's normal. Just create a new reminder. Ask other people in your home to help support you, too.

Designate a hanging file, box, drawer or something that is easily accessible for papers that go with this year's taxes. When you get a tax-related paper, such as a charitable, immediately put it in the hanging file for taxes. Clearly label the spot using color, pictures, or whatever will engage you to know what it is. Again, be creative. Print out a photo of a jail cell and write on it "papers to keep me out of jail!" Working memory and prospective memory (remembering to remember) are common challenges for people with ADHD. Using pneumonic devices such as songs, funny names, and metaphors (the hungry monster garbage/recycle bin) will help make routine tasks more memorable.

Once the action has been taken on papers, eliminate what you can. Note that you have already placed tax-related papers in the tax file. If you still think you want to keep a paper, the easiest solution is to toss it into a box to collect for the year. Write the year's date on the box and start a new box each January. If you have to go back to retrieve something, you can dig through the box. Most of the things people save are never looked at again. How long you save the boxes depends upon what you are storing inside. Try to make good decisions to discard papers right away if you know you don't need it. Ask your CPA, banker, and investments representative what papers to retain. They will know what is best for your particular situation.

Memorabilia is another category of paper that necessities a longer-term storage home. Have an under the bed box to toss your or your child's memory papers and photos in. Make sure it is easy to access the storage bin so memorabilia piles don't stack up in other areas of your house. Be selective about what you keep. Ask yourself if you really want to keep this for later and be honest about whether you will look at it again.

Tips and Tricks for Getting Yourself Going

This is where remembering what you learned in high school physics class comes in handy. Newton's first law states that a body in motion will stay in motion and a body at rest will stay at rest unless acted on by an outside force. When you are in bed or on the couch or sitting and watching television, you have to overcome the laws of motion to get going. That outside force getting you going can be something you set up or include collaboration with another person. Here are some ideas:

Toss Your Phone. Set the alarm on your phone for one minute from now. The more annoying the alarm sounds, the better. Gently toss your phone far enough away that you cannot reach it. When the alarm goes off, you will have to get up to get it. Once you are moving, keep moving towards your destination.

Do a Pull Up. Ask someone else who lives in the house to come next to you, extend his or her hand and help you get up. That person doesn't even need to speak. The outstretched hand is a nonverbal prompt that will cause you to take it automatically.

Phone a Friend. Call someone and ask them to stay on the phone with you until you reach your task. Some people Skype or Facetime with a friend while each of them arrives at and completes a task. Having outside accountability where both of you are active at the same time helps to anchor you to the task even if the other person isn't giving instructions on how to do it.

Use a Body Double. In the same vein as the last strategy, you could have someone physically be in the room with you during the task. This technique is called using a "body double." That other person can be work on a separate task next to you, help you by pre-sorting items that are jumbled, or simply sit there. The only thing the other person should not do is criticize or pester. A body double can be an effective solution to keep you attuned to a task. Consider a child who asks you to help her with homework. She may not require help with answers; instead, she wants your physical presence to stay on task. Try it and you'll see it works. If you need someone to teach you how to do a task, hiring an ADHD organizer or coach is your best bet.

ADDitude magazine (www.attitudemag.com) has weekly articles and tips about ways to manage ADHD symptoms from experts and from people sharing their own tried and true methods. You can search their website to pull up solutions for your challenges.

Danielle's Habit Action Plan

What needs to be done: Keep clothes off the floor and maintain her newly organized closet.

What to do with it: Get her dirty clothes into a hamper and put away clothes after they are clean.

Where to start: The bedroom.

When: Sunday.

Who: Danielle.

Dirty Clothes

Danielle already bought a hamper and placed it halfway between her closet and her bathroom—the two areas where she tended to change clothes. She noticed she did better when the floor was clear because she could see the dirty clothes she forgot to place in the hamper. She also observed that she took off her socks and sweaters in the living room. Rather than expecting that she would walk those clothes to the hamper, she got a second hamper for the living room.

Clean Clothes

When Danielle washed clothes throughout the week, she realized that she forgot to change them from the washer to the dryer. Rather than always having a load to do, she decided to try having Saturday be the day she washed and dried clothes and Sunday be the day she put the clothes away. To keep her anchored to the task on Saturday, Danielle used her kitchen microwave timer to remind her when to switch loads, and she folded clothes while watching her favorite Netflix show. On Sunday, she called her friend Lara to chat while she put away clothes. Lara didn't mind. In fact, Lara used their time to complete routine tasks around her own home.

Danielle gained traction by building her awareness, noting how she tended to do things rather than resorting to immediate self-criticism. She learned this skill while working with the ADHD Specialist Organizer. By creating the separation of herself from the behavior, she saw ways to make her life easier (the hamper in the living room) rather than fighting herself to complete tasks in the so-called right way. She learned what helped her stay focused: having a specific time and day, knowing the first step of her task, and having an outside reminder (the microwave timer) or source of distraction (talking to her friend, watching Netflix). In setting up these components for her most important tasks, Danielle empowered herself to shift her habits instead of interpreting her behaviors as broken and unchangeable. She supported her growth by seeking assistance from people knowledgeable about ADHD. All of these treatment modalities are nudging her towards a more functional place.

Your Turn: Pause & Notice

- In what areas are you trying to mold yourself using unrealistic expectations?
- How can you create systems that are simpler?
- Is there a condition that you suspect you should get checked out by a doctor?
- What from Danielle's story resonated with you?
- What action steps will you take around adapting to a health diagnosis?

Take a photo of an area where you have previously tried to apply willpower and consider why you haven't been successful

Discovery Questions

- Tell me about a time you felt impatient. What was happening? What felt so frustrating? What do you wish you could have changed?
- What was the most miserable time of your life? Why?
- How about the happiest time? What made that different?

CHAPTER 14

Ghosts of Christmas Past

"To everything, there is a season and a time to every purpose under the heaven."
Ecclesiastes 3:1

Mike's Story

Mike felt guilty because he didn't follow through on decorating for Christmas like he used to. For five years, he promised his daughter Rita that he would get everything out, and each year he put it off. Finally, Rita bought him an artificial tabletop tree so at least there would be something festive.

This Christmas, Rita and her husband's eight-month-old baby girl would be having her first Christmas. Rita wondered whether Mike could dress up as Santa and also put up the "real decorations." As much as Mike wanted to carry on their family traditions to a new generation, he just couldn't motivate himself. Getting decorations out was too hard now that Mike's knees were acting up. And he dreaded having to put them away by himself.

For all the years that his wife Deborah was alive, Mike went all out for Christmas. Deborah loved Christmas, and so did Mike. He had a full Santa costume that he wore when delivering presents under the tree. A few times he played Santa at extended family gatherings. He loved bringing joy to others. Deborah loved to decorate trees. Together they decorated about seven each year—six artificial ones of various sizes and one live tree.

The first December that Deborah had cancer, Rita put up one tree and a few other decorations. Their attention was mostly on fighting the disease, staying busy and trying not to think too much about what if's. When the second December arrived, their focus shifted. Doctors said the cancer had progressed too far and they talked about hospice services. The social worker suggested making the most of their time left by revisiting family traditions.

So, Mike, Rita, a few family members, and close friends made an effort to decorate like they used to. On Christmas Eve, Mike sat in his Santa suit next to Deborah's rented hospital bed that was set up in the family room. The white lights from the tree cast a glow on her thin face as she slept. He held her perpetually chilly hands and wept. Deborah died a few days after Christmas.

Mike gave himself a break on decorating for the first couple of years. Instead of staying home, he went to Rita's to celebrate. Things changed once Rita got married, and even more so when she became pregnant. Mike knew how important Christmas was to her and how much he was letting her down. He really didn't love Christmas the way he used to. In fact, he kind of dreaded it. His sweet granddaughter deserved an all-out Christmas. He wanted to get over his procrastination, for her sake.

Pause & Notice

- What problems does Mike see?
- What problems do others see?
- How did elaborate decorating benefit Mike in the past?
- What stands in the way of Mike doing things differently?
- What advice would you give Mike?

Mike's Tipping Point

PAIN OF REMAINING THE SAME	PAIN OF CHANGING	BENEFITS OF CHANGING
Feeling like he's letting his family down by changing	Acknowledging that he cannot continue past traditions as they were	Passing on the most special Christmas things to his daughter
Being overwhelmed by putting up decorations	Taking time to sort decorations	Feeling empowered to set new traditions
Having those piles of decorations taking up space in his home and reminding him of what he needs to do	Going through the decorations will probably bring up emotions, both good and bad	Revisiting memories will reinforce the good times they had
Feeling weighed down by a sense of obligation	Worrying about making a mistake	Someone else can enjoy the decorations they don't want any more
	Having to have an open conversation with his daughter	Feeling unburdened and have a clean space
		Knowing his priorities for continuing certain traditions

Visualize Success

- Success would look like decorations being pared down to an amount that Mike felts capable of doing. Success would mean that his daughter could use some decorations to continue traditions with her own child.

- Success would feel like a more open storage area. Mike would be unburdened from a big job while honoring the past.

Mike's Project Action Plan

What needs to be done: Go through the family Christmas decorations.

What to do with it: Decide what to keep, what to give Rita, and what to donate.

Where to start: Bring a quarter of the holiday boxes upstairs into the family room.

When: Saturday from 9-11 a.m., then additional days as needed.

Who: Mike and his daughter Rita.

Mike will:

- Have the boxes upstairs when Rita arrives;

- Set up a folding table to help with the sorting process;

- Know that the process may create strong emotions, but that Rita is there to support him;

- Go through boxes one at a time, deciding what he would like to keep and letting go of what isn't as meaningful;

- Allow time to tell stories and take photos of items he wants to remember but not keep; and
- Bring the donate boxes into the garage until he and Rita complete the sorting process. This way, he can reclaim items if he changes his mind and add items to the pile if he feels like he is saving too much.

Rita will:
- Make sure she has room in her car to bring things home;
- Bring over bubble wrap to rewrap fragile items;
- Know that the process may create strong emotions and that her father is there to support her;
- Identify items that are most meaningful to her that she would like to keep;
- Take what she is keeping home with her; and
- Load up donations at the end of the process and drop them off.

When Zombies Attack

Opening the Box

When difficult things happen, it is easy to fall into faulty thought patterns. One such pattern is all-or-nothing thinking. For Mike, the choices felt like either going all out decorating for Christmas or doing nothing. There was a third choice, however, one that carried forward the aspects that he still enjoyed while letting go of the parts that felt cumbersome. Before Mike could figure out a third way, he needed to stop resisting. Objects that carry deep significance carry energy—both positive and negative—and that could feel scary.

I'll never forget the time I assisted a client to sort storage tubs that had been sealed for years. The tubs contained old letters, obituaries, junk mail, diaries, and miscellaneous objects that had been swooped up because of a quick move. We were working in a small basement room. After about two hours of sorting, we both noticed that we felt emotional, even crying at times. We remarked on how heavy the air felt. All of a sudden, I realized our mistake of going through such energy-filled stuff in an enclosed space. Fortunately, there were windows in the room to let fresh air inside. We also grabbed a diffuser and added Thieves essential oil. What a difference that made! Since then, I'm careful to set up an environment that circulates the air or to bring the bins in small batches to a more open space. Maybe this sounds wacky to you, but it does help those of us sensitive to energy.

I've helped many people to process a deceased loved one's belongings. Sometimes the things you would expect to bring up strong emotions do. Other times it's the unexpected objects that pack an emotional punch, like the smell of pipe smoke on a shirt, or papers from the trip you had to cancel, or the ugly keychain your loved one carried around. Having another person there offers comfort simply through his presence. A support person shares laughter, too, willingly listening because stories are our way to consciously sift through what has happened and to acknowledge its reality. Being a support person gives a precious gift to a grieving person.

Overcoming Overwhelm

Imagine standing at the door of your packed storage room. You want to run away. You'd rather clean mildew off the bathroom tile than tackle the boxes and bins in front of you. A stream of all-or-nothing thoughts fills your mind: *All of this is junk. I need to get a dumpster. All of this is probably stuff I want to keep, but I know I shouldn't. It's going to be so hard. Can I deal with this today? I cannot deal with this today. I should deal with this today. Where do I even start?*

First, let me assure you that the bins in front of you are not equal. I have never had a client go through items one by one and end up keeping everything or throwing it all away. Once you start sorting, you will discover that you have keepers, tossers, and the muddle in-between. You just need to start. Here are some techniques for overcoming that overwhelmed feeling:

- Pull a box from the room to sort in another room;
- Start on the left and work your way around the room to the right;
- Start with what's out in the center or on the floor;
- Go on a hunt for all the trash in the room, or empty boxes, or one category of items, or things that are blue. It really doesn't matter how you narrow it as long as narrowing it helps you focus;
- Decide on the big pieces in the room first;
- If you tend to get visually overwhelmed, cover what you are not sorting with a plain bed sheet;
- Enlist help from another person to pre-sort the mixed-up items (and tell the helper he is not allowed to comment on the contents or your decisions);
- Set a timer for fifteen minutes. You can do anything for fifteen minutes;

- Post your goal for the day on the wall: "two boxes sorted" or "get through all the old magazines;"
- Use techniques from the getting started tips in Chapter 13; or
- Each day find fifteen things to donate.

Circle the one that you will try doing first when you get overwhelmed.

Exploring New Possibilities

When you find yourself stuck and resistant, the first thing to do is to make a list, or, if you are a verbal processor, to speak it out loud and have another person make notes. Your list will cover everything on your mind. Mike's list might include writing down all of the ways that he and Deborah decorated, the holiday traditions that were most special to them, things that he remembers, what he is worried about, what feels hard, and what feels easy. Until he gets the chaos swirling in his brain out, he doesn't have room to consider other possibilities. If you skip this step, you may find yourself stuck. No worries, you still can make a list.

I think of that swirling chaos like a wall that is blocking my view. I cannot see around the wall. The wall is there. Once I acknowledge the existence of the wall and what it is made from, I can deconstruct it. When the wall is down, or mostly down, I'm suddenly able to see beyond it. This can happen for Mike. Once he goes through the writing or talking process, he can begin to consider which traditions he wants to continue, imagine how his daughter could enjoy having some of the decorations and decide on new ways to celebrate Christmas.

Throughout their lifetimes, most people change how they decorate for seasons and holidays. Seeing the excitement of a child enjoying decorations motivates adults to put effort into holiday celebrations. Once children grow up, the effort of moving boxes from storage, setting out and taking down decorations often begins to feel like more of a burden than a joy. Adults may continue decorating at the same level because that's the way they've always done it, regardless of how much or how little they enjoy the process and the result. But they don't have to.

Holiday decorating is a prime example of when you can realign your desires, your life stage, and your stuff. If the thrill of holiday decorating is gone, let it go. Reinvent your habits. You can scale back how much you do, you can completely eliminate decorating for a holiday, or you can replace it with something new. Scale back by challenging yourself to reduce items for a holiday by half or more. Eliminate decorating for holidays that feel like a burden. You can combine these ideas by choosing just a couple of spots to decorate—such as a door wreath or the top of a buffet cabinet—and display by season instead of holiday. For example, use general Fall decor rather than ones specific to Halloween and Thanksgiving.

To replace previous decorating habits with something new, first ask yourself, "What do I love about decorating for this holiday?" If the answer is that you love to express creativity by transforming a space, but you only enjoy it if others enjoy it, then consider how else you might fill that need. Would a local club or senior center appreciate someone decorating for that holiday? By discovering what personal interests motivate you, you can find that joy in a different way than what you have done in the past. You aren't abandoning the tradition; you are merely shifting your efforts to where you can still feel satisfied.

Mike's Habit Action Plan

What needs to be done: Implement his new traditions and follow through on doing the ones he will continue.

What to do with it: Make a list of past traditions and talk to his daughter about her own wishes, and then consider how he wants to move forward.

Where to start: List all the ways he and his wife decorated for Christmas in the past and their favorite traditions.

When: Wednesday after lunch.

Who: Mike.

Mike will:

- Brainstorm a list of all the ways they decorated, room by room;
- Write down fond memories of their traditions;
- Call his daughter and ask her to share her favorite memories;
- Ask her what traditions she plans to continue and whether she has requests for him to continue certain traditions;
- Create another list of possible traditions to carry on;
- Choose 2-3 traditions to continue this Christmas;
- Do those things and notice if it brings him joy or not; and
- Know that he can change his mind and habits along the way.

Your Turn: Pause & Notice

- What have been your favorite holidays to decorate for?
- Have you noticed your interest in decorating has changed?

- What are the things you enjoy most about decorating for your favorite holiday?
- What aspects do you no longer enjoy?
- What are other ways you could carry forward the aspects that you enjoy?
- What action steps will you take around holiday decorations?

Take a photo of your holiday storage area.

Discovery Questions

- Tell me a story about yourself that you love to tell.
- What makes this story so special?
- What qualities does the story highlight?
- Is there a "moral of the story" that would benefit others to know?

CHAPTER 15

What is Possible for Helen

"People don't cry when they lose their hope. They cry when they get it back."
Martha Beck

Helen's Story

Helen thought of herself as a nice person, so she was a little surprised by her angry reaction when she received an invitation to her friend's fiftieth wedding anniversary—just a month before she would have celebrated her fiftieth with her husband, Joe. Seven years had passed since he died, which felt both like forever and no time at all.

Most of Helen's friends had moved into condos or smaller houses from the homes where they raised their children. Some had moved away. Others were snowbirds. Helen really couldn't keep up with her big house and yard. She hired out her yard work because the neighbors would complain if she let it go, but she thought she should be able to get the housework done alone. When the dust and clutter built up, she took a break from hosting her bridge group.

As much as her home connected her to Joe's memory, she also felt terribly lonely. She rarely cooked. Mostly, she picked up food in a drive-thru and ate in front of the television. The TV was her constant companion. She only turned it off at night after she had fallen asleep in the recliner, woken up, and decided to move to her bed.

Her daughter, Sarah, encouraged Helen to move to a senior living community because she would have more company there and meals would be provided. It sounded pretty good to Helen until the reality of having to go through her house hit her. When Sarah offered to help her, Helen admitted she wasn't quite ready. Six months after Joe's death, Sarah had helped to remove his clothing from the master bedroom closet, they both ended up sobbing. Sarah took the clothes for donation and Helen climbed into bed and slept for eighteen hours. Helen didn't think she could handle that again. So, she did nothing.

It might have been different if Helen could talk to her friends about what she felt, but they all still had living husbands. Even the ones who had divorced were remarried. Helen was the only single person in her friend group. No one asked her to stop coming to their dinner parties, but she did.

Helen stumbled upon an online article suggesting ways to overcome loneliness. One of the challenges was to go to a movie, even if that meant going alone. She summoned the courage to go see one of the Academy Award-nominated dramas which had been in the theaters for quite a while. As she sat down with her popcorn, she noticed another solitary soul a few rows ahead. Before she could change her mind, Helen approached the woman and struck up a conversation. Turned out, they were both widows. After the movie, they went to a café and chatted for two hours. They made plans to meet again.

When Helen returned to her home that evening, it felt like she was seeing her house for the first time. There were little piles all around. The floor needed vacuuming. She smelled something sour coming from the kitchen. "Why in the world am I living like this?" she wondered.

Your Turn: Pause & Notice

- What problems does Helen see?
- What problems do others see?
- Why would meeting a new friend make a difference to Helen?
- What stands in the way of Helen doing things differently?
- What advice would you give Helen?

Helen's Tipping Point

PAIN OF REMAINING THE SAME	PAIN OF CHANGING	BENEFITS OF CHANGING
Keeping herself stuck in her old life	Figuring out how to make changes	Seeing the possibilities of future happiness
Continuing to take poor care of herself	Investigating whether she needs additional support	Getting the help she needs means not having to do it alone
Continuing to feel lonely and isolated	Taking the chance to be vulnerable to trying new things	Feeling the exhilaration of trying new things
Having to outsource home tasks because she cannot do them		Not having such a big house to take care of
		Feeling excited to spend time with new friends

Visualize Success

- Success would look like moving to a place where she wouldn't have to manage the upkeep, someone else would make meals, and she would interact with others socially.
- Success would feel like a sense of ease in her day-to-day living, connecting to others, and feeling like part of a community.

Helen's Project Action Plan

What needs to be done: Downsize from her house to a two-bedroom unit in the independent living section of a continuous care retirement community.

What to do with it: Decide on the activities that she currently enjoys, the belongings that she currently uses, and have an estate sale of the rest. Her new space will be seventy percent smaller than her family home, so she needs to reduce her possessions by as close to seventy percent as she can get.

Where to start: Get a floor plan of her new home.

When: Tuesday at 9 a.m. and additional days.

Who: Helen, her daughter Sarah, and Angela, a Senior Move Manager.

A Senior Move Manager® specializes in helping people downsize, move, and set up at the new location. They can assist with some or all aspects involved in a move or suggest resources, such as estate sale companies, movers, haulers, and handymen, to complete those aspects. The first step of the process involves meeting to determine a clients' needs, timeline, and overall project plan, including what resources are required to complete the job and what homeowners will do. People with limited mobility, with children who live far away and/or do not want to help, those who are on tight schedule, or who simply want a smoother transition will benefit from having assistance in all or most aspects of the process. Another option, NASMM@HOME, connects Senior Move Managers® to people who want to age in place. Find a Senior Move Manager near you through the National Association of Senior Move Managers at https://www.nasmm.org or by calling 877-606-2766.

In Helen's case, Helen, daughter Sarah, and Senior Move Manager Angela have already identified Helen's goals and established a timeline. They have chosen resources for packing and moving what Helen has selected; holding an estate sale for what is not selected; hauling away what remains after the sale; and painting, repairing, and readying the house for sale. The Senior Move Manager and her team will assist Helen with space planning for her move, sort through the belongings, coordinate with the other resources, and unpack Helen at her new home.

Helen will:
- Create a list of hobbies and activities she still enjoys;
- Think through what kitchen items she will actually use considering that her meals will be mostly provided;
- Go through her clothing with Sarah to identify what fits, what is in good condition, and what she loves wearing;
- Sort through her jewelry with Sarah, giving Sarah first choice on jewelry she will otherwise sell;
- Keep only the toiletries she uses and likes;
- Consider getting new bed and bath linens for her new home;

- Choose her favorite books and knick-knacks, with Sarah taking photos of things she does not want to keep, but wants to remember; and
- Go through memorabilia and photos with Sarah.

Sarah will:

- Go through her own items that have been stored in her mother's home;
- Help to gather the hobby items her mother wants to keep;
- Show kindness to her mother by being patient, avoiding criticism, and taking her own breaks when she feels overwhelmed by the process; and
- Assist the team in going through papers per Helen's rules of what can be shredded or recycled.

Angela will:

- Assist Helen in filling out the pre-move checklist (see below), taking measurements and strategizing the space planning;
- Create a master list of what furnishings will be moved;
- Act as project manager, meaning she will be the point person who communicates with Helen;
- Use the pre-move checklist as a guide for her team; and
- Encourage Helen, reminding her of her goals to have a comfortable, but not crowded new home.

Angela's team will:

- Create a staging area for items that will be moved;

- Discard items that Helen has approved to be discarded, such as expired food and junk mail; and
- Pre-sort items into categories to make Helen's decisions easier.

Pre-Move Checklist

Step One: Gather information

- ❏ Find out what amenities the continuous care community provides (weekly cleaning, laundry, ironing, meal service, paper products, handyman service) so that she knows what she will not have to bring.
- ❏ Get the floorplan of the new home.
- ❏ Measure furniture and decide what will comfortably fit into new space. Is the scale of her current furniture too large for the smaller rooms?
- ❏ Assess whether the floorplan has space to display decorative pieces and books. How many inches are available for books and knick-knacks?
- ❏ How much lighting will she want?
- ❏ Sketch the furniture placement on the floorplan.
- ❏ Measure new closet space in inches to determine how many clothes can fit comfortably in the new closet.
- ❏ Measure cabinet space in the kitchenette.
- ❏ Determine when she will use her kitchenette (i.e. for breakfast, to hold snacks, to have a friend over for coffee or tea) to know what she will or will not need to bring.
- ❏ Measure space in the new bathroom.
- ❏ Decide if she needs an additional shelf above the toilet.

❑ Will she keep her current bed and bath linens or get new ones?

Step Two: Use measurements to choose what to bring

❑ Mark furniture, rugs, and lamps that will be moved.

❑ Assess "soft items" like clothing, shoes, and outerwear, as well as blankets, bedding, pillows, towels, and rugs.

❑ Assess jewelry.

❑ Assess bath items, toiletries, hair products.

❑ Assess kitchen items and food.

❑ Assess books and magazines.

❑ Assess decorative items such as knick-knacks, collections, candles, handing pictures, art, and wall items.

❑ Assess seasonal decorations, knowing there will be very little space for these items.

❑ Assess gift wrap and greeting cards.

❑ Assess current hobby interests and streamline the supplies.

❑ Assess board games.

❑ Assess desk supplies (pens, stapler, paper clips, etc.).

❑ Assess financial papers and files.

❑ Assess electronics, CDs, and DVDs.

❑ Assess tools. Is this provided? Assemble a small toolkit?

❑ Assess gardening supplies, plants, and outdoor recreation.

❑ Assess cleaning supplies. Is this provided?

❑ Assess other boxes that have been stored in the basement or attic.

❑ Assess miscellaneous stuff that has been gathered from around the house.

❑ Assess memorabilia and photos at least to make the first elimination, and then be more meticulous post-move.

Step Three: Complete other tasks

❑ Purchase items she wants in the new home.

❑ Give certain items to specific people (family, friends, organizations).

❑ Work through any follow-up tasks that will allow her to streamline her stuff, such as paper or photo scanning, digitizing music, etc.

❑ Get moved in and either bring items back to include in the sale or pull items from the sell pile that she didn't realize she would use (limit this!). Most likely she will have moved too much, and she can use this opportunity to put the extra stuff back in the sale.

When Zombies Attack

Be Brave! Follow Nudges

Helen had been in a holding pattern for a long time, one that she would have continued if she hadn't noticed her strong feelings about her friend's anniversary and if she had chickened out on talking to the stranger at the theater. Instead, Helen acted bravely.

Behaving differently could feel out of control, but that doesn't necessarily mean you are on the wrong path. (Just to be clear, I'm not talking about illicit, illegal, or immoral actions.) It means you are experimenting. I'll never forget when a very mild-mannered friend of mine got upset because the group wasn't listening to the request of one group member.

"Listen!" she said, "What he is asking us to do isn't a big deal. Let's just do it."

Everyone fell into line after that.

Afterwards, I could tell she was a bit shaky, so I asked if she was okay.

"I feel really awful," she explained. "How could I yell like that? People are probably upset with me!"

I was shocked to hear she thought she was yelling because her voice was as loud as most people normally talk and her words were not unkind or aggressive. But to her, the volume and tone of her words felt like she was shouting.

"No one is upset with you," I reassured her. "It may have felt like you were yelling, but no one else felt that way. We weren't listening to his request until you stood up for him."

"They weren't listening! That made me so mad. I don't usually say anything, but I had to!" she replied.

"It took a lot of courage for you to say something, didn't it?"

"Yes, and I feel really awful, like I was out of control."

"Of course you felt out of control," I said. "You were trying something new. It's normal to feel uncomfortable and like you need to figure out the right words or the right volume."

She nodded, and I could tell she was still considering whether or not she had done the right thing.

"How would you have felt if you hadn't said anything?" I asked.

"Terrible."

"Worse than you feel now?"

"Definitely," she said. "I would have been angry about it for a long time."

"But instead you were brave, and you tried something different."

"I did." She repeatedly nodded as though the thought was sinking in. "I did, and I'm glad I said something even though this feels weird."

Both my friend and Helen felt nudges to act differently. I have no idea how many times in the past my friend had kept silent due to fear. Similarly, Helen probably had many days where she felt lonely, upset at how her life had changed, and overwhelmed by the thought of doing something besides the status quo of surviving. Everyone has their own timetable for processing change and grief. Gradually, you may find yourself feeling more nudges to shift. This means you are getting ready to be brave. You aren't going to be a hundred percent ready for anything. I'd venture to say that most people show up afraid. That's normal.

Helen may not have realized it, but she had been nurturing her bravery by reading about and noticing articles on how to find social connections. Going to a movie alone seemed like a risk because it was outside of her comfort zone. Remember what's normal to feel when you take actions that are outside your comfort zone? That's right—you might feel uncomfortable, and maybe a bit daring or exhilarated. When you take these risks, who are you being? You are the person who is adventurous, the person who makes things happen, and the person who is the hero of her own story.

Do Something Silly or Weird Every Day

If you are someone who tends to overthink situations, then get some practice with loosening up. Over the next month, do something silly or weird each day, which means doing what feels out of character for you, edgy, daring, and exciting. Below are some ideas to get started. Please add your own. To discover more ideas, finish the sentence: "I would never let myself do these things..."

- Burst into song at the grocery store
- Eat at a restaurant alone
- Put on two different shoes
- Start a conversation with a stranger
- Apply a temporary tattoo to your forearm and see how long it takes before someone says something
- Pretend to be someone famous dressed incognito
- Go to a café or bar to listen to Jazz
- Take a comedy improv class
- Bounce a rubber ball
- Visit your local zoo
- Wear a Halloween costume on a normal day
- Deliver flowers to your dentist
- Paint your fingernails black
- Eat a food you have never tried
- Talk with a fake accent
- Wear a swimsuit around the house in winter
- Play a children's game like Candyland with an adult friend
- Temporarily dye your hair with Kool-Aid
- Anonymously pay for someone else's meal or drive-through order
- What would you add to this list?

Gather Info Now

A big process like downsizing works better when you have help and plan ahead. Even if you are not quite ready to move, you can take some preliminary steps now that will pay off later.

Tour different kinds of "next homes," such as continuous care retirement communities that offer independent living to assisted living and skilled care, condos where you don't have to do outside yard work, and apartment buildings geared towards older adults. Even if you plan to move to a different city to be near a loved one, these tours will help you get the flavor of different options and begin to visualize how your stuff might fit into the layouts, as well as get familiar with the amenities offered. Ask friends who have moved for tips on what they like or dislike about their choices. Use the floor plans from these tours to estimate what furnishings you could take with you.

Make a list of repairs, room by room, to be done to sell your home. Consult with realtors on what updates should be made for your house to be marketable and how you can be most strategic with spending money on home updates. Take a couple of Sundays to tour open houses in your area to get a sense of what's on the market. The realtors you consult can give you an idea of what your home might sell for, what's a good time of year to list it, and tips for getting a fast sale. Ask the realtors and your friends for recommendations for service people that can do necessary repairs and updates.

Identify valuable items you might sell. Research their value on eBay (see Chapter 3). Visit local resale or antique shops to see what similar items are selling for and talk to the shop owner about your object. Search on Google for "selling [your item]." Often there are individuals or companies who specialize in selling a particular kind of object. Contact them with information on your collection. They will have the best idea of its market value now. Perhaps, after taking these steps, you realize you need an appraisal. An appraisal from years ago is not going to reflect the current market. As I discussed in Chapter 3, the market for many items has substantially decreased. It may take time for this reality to sink in. When it comes time for you to sell what you aren't taking with you, you will have a realistic measure of what items will sell for.

Talk to friends who have had estate sales or auctions to find out whom they recommend using (or even staying away from). Attend some of these sales to know how they run. Interview potential sale providers to find out whether you could have a profitable sale, or if donating your goods would be more beneficial.

Identify what you love to do the most, how you do and do not want to spend your time, and begin to downsize your home to support those goals. If you find you are not following through on the process, contact professional organizers, Senior Move Managers® or other professionals to help with the process. By working on decision-making over a longer period of time, such as a year, you will be able to rest and not overdo it mentally or physically.

Helen's Habit Action Plan

What needs to be done: Feel more zest with life.

What to do with it: Get out of her comfort zone by trying different things.

Where to start: By doing the thirty-day challenge to try something silly and weird.

When: On the first day of the next month.

Who: Helen and her new friend, who was also excited about the challenge.

Helen will:

- Come up with thirty silly and weird things that she can try;
- Write each one on a slip of paper;
- Place the papers into a bowl;
- Draw one each day and do it;
- Keep a journal with at least one entry per week that describes how the challenge is going; and
- Compare notes to see how her friend's challenge is going.

Your Turn: Pause & Notice

- What kind of "next home" do you envision yourself moving to?
- If you have considered moving to a smaller place, what would make the change worthwhile? What would you be gaining?
- What would you be excited to not have to do anymore?
- What concerns would you have about making this transition?
- What would help you get through a big project like downsizing a home?
- What resources might you need (move manager, organizer, moving company, handyman, estate sale person, etc.)?
- What category of things feels easiest to start sorting?

Take a photo of each room of your house.

Discovery Questions

- What's a challenge you are going through now? What advice would you give to a friend if she were going through this same situation?
- Is that advice different than how you are handling it? What would keep you from taking that advice?

CHAPTER 16

Create Your Life's Instruction Manual

"Just don't give up trying to do what you really want to do.
Where there is love and inspiration, I don't think you can go wrong."
Ella Fitzgerald

The Process of Realignment

We covered a lot of ground, haven't we? This final chapter brings together some of the biggest takeaways within these pages and reminds you of how these pieces fit together in the puzzle of realignment. The illustration below will help to summarize the book's key concepts.

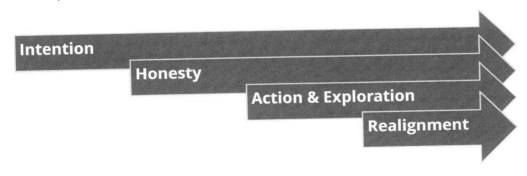

Choose Your Intention

By now, you know that the realignment process doesn't start with buying containers or even the idea that you should get rid of stuff; it begins with your mindset. Will you continue to turn a blind eye to ways your life isn't functioning or will you take an active role as the hero of your life? This is the first, and most crucial, decision.

I have spent a lot of time discussing life transitions, which can be anticipated or unanticipated, normative or non-normative, but which all of us experience, whether we like it or not. You don't get a choice about having to navigate changes in life, but you do get to choose how you react to what happens.

Getting through life transitions requires skills that you may not have been taught. Bridge's Transition Model (in Chapter 6) demonstrates how emotions dominate life transitions. Those strong emotions can be intimidating if you don't know how to lean into, rather than run away from, them. Choosing to be the hero of your life means choosing to show up afraid and responding to the situation as it unfolds. It means facing the truth of what you see and leveraging your inner strength even as you worry whether you are strong enough.

If you commit to the process, you will discover how resilient and resourceful you really are. You will be an active participant committed to the process of acknowledging and accepting your life as it is right now. Noting what *is* happening helps you control your life as much as possible. When you avoid facing the truth, you give away your chance to react in a truly empowered way.

You can have the life you want, but you must stop trying to go it alone. Commit to the intention of getting support from friends and professionals, from books, videos, and experts. No hero succeeds alone, and you don't either.

Be Honest about Your Knowledge, Life Stage, and Stuff

Once you have set your intention to actively evaluate your life, you begin the process of gathering information about it. This means taking a fresh look at your knowledge, your life stage, and your stuff. Your knowledge includes what skills you currently have and your habits in managing life. It's likely that your skills and habits need tweaking in response to an honest assessment of your life stage.

Honesty requires a few things: building self-awareness, having enough curiosity to question the status quo, and a willingness to experiment. The first part, building self-awareness, consists of you learning how to observe your behavior, the internal chattering about that behavior, and to consciously notice what is happening. Awareness is the building block for success. It inserts a pause into otherwise automatic actions and it separates you, as a person, from the nasty thoughts you say about yourself.

Your emerging awareness gives you strength to question the status quo, unexamined assumptions, and unconscious habits. You get to be a rebel with a cause: your well-being. Questioning assumptions and roles means you get to be the boss of your life—not tradition, not fear of what ifs, or anything else that's been keeping you stuck.

From here you will try new ways of doing things, experimenting with what uniquely works for you. You'll notice how your experiments turn out, then tweak them some more, until you circle around to a realigned life. It's amazingly empowering, and kind of fun, to be your own life's scientist.

Don't isolate yourself in the process of honestly evaluating your life stage. How many of your friends are going through the same thing and not talking about it? Sure, they may complain about aches and pains, but are they talking about the deeper stuff? Enlist companions who can be sounding boards, offer other perspectives, and lift you up with their support. If you cannot think of friends who are good listeners, then hire a coach or therapist to hold open a sacred space for you to process.

When you tell the truth about your life stage, you become alert to how your knowledge (skills and habits) were matched with a different life stage, and what that means for your stuff. You probably don't need to shop in bulk if you cook for two. Perhaps your print books can be donated if you only listen to audiobooks. Throughout the book, I've presented truth-testing ideas, such as taking a "before" photo of your space, estimating an item's value using eBay, and setting an expiration date for "wish clothing." As you practice trust-testing, it will get easier to accept what you see, especially when paired with building your awareness without the negative self-talk.

Take Action and Explore Possibilities

When you opened this book, you probably thought action would be the starting point. I hope you can see why it comes after setting your intention and observing your life honestly. In this part of the process, you get through the backlog of stuff and set up new structures. That's only possible because you know better what you need for your circumstances now. It's hard to pack for a trip if you don't know where you are going. Now that you have a sense of where you are going, you can decide what to bring along.

The components of taking action are being specific, using strategies, and enlisting support. Fuzzy goals undermine getting things done. As I said at the beginning, you will not get projects accomplished until you choose a specific date and time, and recruit someone else who will check-in to see if you followed through. This accountability acts like a scaffold around a house that's under construction. It's a non-negotiable component. I've modeled accountability in the Project and Habit Action Plans throughout the book. Defining what success looks and feels like marks another key part of being specific. How will you know you are finished if you haven't articulated what that will be? Being specific with your starting place helps you to overcome initially feeling overwhelmed when you stand at the doorway of a big project. Chapter 14 has a list of potential starting spots.

What strategies within the book have been most helpful for you? Many people struggle with knowing how to let go of sentimental belongings or ones they have inherited. To start with, letting go involves challenging your assumptions about having to keep items forever. Each thing has a life cycle. It may be as short as eating a piece of chocolate or as long as carrying an object with you until you die. Perhaps a belonging's life cycle is somewhere in the middle. You can still honor an item regardless of its life cycle. There are many ways to honor precious items, such as taking a photo, journaling its history, or making it into something new, like a t-shirt quilt. Creating a letting go ritual with these techniques or by expressing gratitude allows you to make decisions that align with who you are now.

The notion of self-help troubles me. We really are better off when we have friends and experts to support our efforts. Each scenario in this book had a plan that included helpers. I didn't include that for selfish reasons. I did it because having the right helper gets you from overwhelmed to finished. There are many kinds of helpers to use during the action stage, including professional organizers, life coaches, move managers, photo organizers, as well as supportive friends and family. Had you heard about the concept of a body double before reading this book? It's not glorified babysitting; it's a powerful strategy to use in the action stage. Support happens outside of the project work too. People in the scenarios enlisted help from individual and marriage therapists, professionals trained in Harm Reduction and Cognitive Behavioral Therapy, and ADHD. The bottom line is that you get the assistance you need, no matter what form it takes.

While you take action to process your belongings, you explore who you are now based on revisiting who you have been in the past and the values that determine who you want to be in the future. Your truth-telling and awareness have laid the groundwork for you to consider what excites you in this life stage. What hobbies and activities are on your bucket list? How can you apply abilities gained during your career to other venues? The discovery questions in each chapter prompt reflection about what's most important to you, alert you to areas of regret, show you opportunities to resolve old conflicts and remind you of the highs and lows of your life story. Finding what David Solie calls your "organic legacy" (Chapter 11) marks *the* developmental task of aging.

Realign Your Home and Life

What began as an intentional commitment to evaluating your knowledge, life stage, and stuff with honesty is what allowed you to take action to create a new vision for your next stage. That vision isn't totally new, though. It is based on everything that came before it—the good, bad, and the middle-ish. This process isn't about fixing you or starting fresh; instead, the realignment process seeks to mine your experiences, build on your strengths, and honor the value that is *already there*. The goal of realignment is to live a joyful life where your belongings serve you and your solutions fit what you can maintain.

Create the Instruction Manual for You

If you have been an active participant throughout these chapters, then you have come to understand or reaffirm what does and does not help you find joy. Did you realize you were writing your personal instruction manual? The journaling you have done to fill out each chapter's exercises, to answer the discovery questions, and to create action plans capture pieces of your personal instruction manual. This is a document you can refer to when you design new systems and tackle projects. There are a couple of other areas to add:

- What time of day do you have the most energy? The least?
- How busy do you like to be?
- What's your morning routine?
- What's your bedtime routine?
- How do you like to learn—by seeing, hearing, touching, or being in motion?
- What do you already know about taking care of yourself?
- What strategies in this book worked for you the best?
- What helps you get started?
- Who helps you the most to persevere?
- Where are you in the realignment process and where do you plan to go next?

Tracking Your Progress

Below are two checklists. The first shows areas that were covered in the book's chapters. The second marks additional areas of your home that may require attention. Use these as a way to track the progress of your home alignment. Add additional rooms or areas if you don't see them listed already.

Mark which areas you worked on from the chapters:

- ❑ Kitchen
- ❑ Pantry
- ❑ Recipes and Cookbooks
- ❑ Magazines/Newspapers/Catalogs
- ❑ Collections
- ❑ Gift Wrap
- ❑ Gift Stockpile
- ❑ Bath Products
- ❑ Books
- ❑ Papers/Supplies Related to Your Career

- ❑ Clothes Closet
- ❑ Memory Clothes
- ❑ Tools
- ❑ Garage Items
- ❑ Photos
- ❑ Memorabilia
- ❑ Inherited Items
- ❑ Sentimental Items
- ❑ Laundry System
- ❑ Mail
- ❑ Seasonal Decorations
- ❑ Hobby Supplies

Here are additional areas found in most homes to supplement the list above:

- ❑ Living Room
- ❑ CDs/DVDs
- ❑ Knick-Knacks
- ❑ Dining Room
- ❑ Tablecloths/Napkins
- ❑ Fine China/Stemware
- ❑ Junk Drawer(s)
- ❑ Entry Closet/Mudroom
- ❑ Bathroom #1
- ❑ Bathroom #2
- ❑ Bathroom #3

- ❑ Bedroom #1
- ❑ Bedroom #2
- ❑ Bedroom #3
- ❑ Bedroom #4
- ❑ Linen Closet
- ❑ Toy Area
- ❑ Hobby Room
- ❑ Attic
- ❑ Utility Room
- ❑ Garden Supplies
- ❑ Sports Equipment
- ❑ Camping Equipment

You Did It!

I am so proud of the work you have put into this, and the attention and intention you have placed upon your well-being. Who did you need to be to take this journey? Brave, persistent, resilience, resourceful are just a few words that come to my mind. Go back to the end of Chapter 1 and read the letter you wrote to yourself. How does who you were then compare to who you are now?

It has been a privilege to be part of your self-discovery journey. I'd love to continue to support you and get feedback on what has been most useful about this book. My email is kate@greenlightorganizing.com. Visit www.DiscoverWhoAmiNow.com or www.KateVarness.com for the additional book resources, as well as encouragement and inspiration via my blog. I wish you all the best as you step bravely forward.

xoxo,

Kate

Appendix A – Blank Forms

Your Tipping Point

PAIN OF REMAINING THE SAME	PAIN OF CHANGING	BENEFITS OF CHANGING

Your Project Action Plan

What needs to be done:

What to do with it:

Where to start:

When:

Who:

You will:

The helper will:

Your Habit Action Plan

What needs to be done:

What to do with it:

Where to start:

When:

Who:

You will:

The helper will:

Appendix B – Work with a Partner or Group

Here's the deal. You don't even realize how ineffective it is to try to work on your own. That's not a personal criticism. It has nothing to do with your level of discipline. It's more that you don't know what you don't know. Once you have been part of a peer group that is effectively run or you have found an accountability partner, you realize the benefits, such as:

- Hearing other people verbalize your secret thoughts;
- Realizing that you are the only one who struggles;
- Being inspired by how someone else has made a small improvement;
- Knowing that everyone is there to support each other, so it is safe to be vulnerable and truthful;
- Having people listen to you with interest;
- Honoring that specific time and day to work through the materials;
- Connecting with others rather than being isolated; and
- Not feeling like the burden is all on your shoulders.

You certainly can complete this book on your own. But what if you tried working through it with a partner, or a small group?

How do you find a partner or a small group (four people or less)? Hint: silently hoping someone will read your mind won't get you anywhere. You will need to talk to other people, but it may not be as hard as you anticipate. Next time you are with your friends, mention that you bought this book and that the author says it's really good to have a partner to work through it. Ask, "Do you know anyone who needs to reduce clutter and figure out what they need to keep for their current life?" Just keep asking individuals until you find someone who seems most invested in following through.

Explain that you will be working through two chapters a month (or whatever pace you decide) and that you want a partner who will read the chapter, complete the exercises, and get together to talk about it for one hour every Sunday afternoon (or whatever fits your schedules). During your weekly meeting, you can review how the previous week's goals went, discuss chapter material, and set your goals for what you will try during the coming week,

It's very important for you and your partner/small group to have some basic agreements.

1) What you share in the group is confidential and not to be shared with people not in the group.

2) Focus more on solving your own problems than on giving the other person advice. Why? Because when you give advice to others, you are avoiding your own issues. Also, very few people want to receive advice. It's much more powerful to discover within yourself how to solve your own problems.

3) Be curious about what others are saying and ask follow-up questions. Good questions include, "What do you already know about doing ____?" and "How can I support you?"

4) Each person will show up for the time you have set aside. If one person repeatedly does not show up, he or she may not be ready for this process. That's okay. You can find another partner. Agree that if you have to reschedule three times, that means you are moving on to another partner. Do not waste your opportunity to make positive changes in your life on someone who is not ready. Their behavior is not about you. Honor their stage in the process and your own.

5) Do the exercises. It may bring up uncomfortable feelings. Remember that indicates you are on track and that you are doing the work necessary to have a life that works for who you are now.

6) Get clear on how each of you will react when homework is and is not completed.

- How does your partner/group member want you to react when they have completed their homework? (For example, doing a happy dance, letting out a cheer, asking what things made getting it done possible.)

- How do they want you to react when they do not complete their homework? (For example, reminding them of their original goals, asking what got in the way, brainstorming ways to aid completion, finding out what they learned from not getting it done.)

7) Speak up to maintain the integrity of the group. By harboring hurt feelings, you undermine your own process. Some ideas for how to word it:

- If you feel hurt by someone's comment, say, "I'm sure you didn't mean to hurt my feelings, but when you said that, it made me feel bad."

- If someone is constantly giving advice, say, "I'm noticing that you seem to be really interested in solving other people's challenges. What advice would you give to yourself?"

- If you hear that a group member broke confidentiality, say, "We cannot have an effective group where everyone feels safe to share if things aren't confidential. Those who cannot honor our confidentiality agreement cannot stay in the group."

- If someone's response continuously feels unhelpful, say, "I appreciate your support. The best way to support me is ___ (to ask a question, let me finish my story, put your phone in your purse so I know I have your full attention, etc.)

Just because I have covered these scenarios, doesn't mean you will encounter them. Persevere to find a partner so that you reinforce your commitment to making real change. Because I recognize that managing group dynamics takes more energy than some people have, I will be running small groups based on this book. Find out when the next one begins by looking at www.DiscoverWhoAmiNow.com.

Study Group Agreements

1. I will keep what is shared in the group confidential.

2. I will focus more on solving my own problems rather than give advice.

3. I will be curious about what others say and ask follow-up questions.

4. I will show up on time on the agreed weekly date.

5. I will do the exercises in each chapter.

6. I will ask for clarification on how to respond when another person does or does not complete homework.

7. I will speak up for myself and ask for what I need.

Signed: _____   Date: _____

Resources

Find an ADHD Coach

ADD Coach Academy
https://addca.com/adhd-coach-training/ADHD-Coaches/

Professional Association for ADHD Coaches
https://paaccoaches.org/find-an-adhd-coach/

Find an Organizer Coach

Coach Approach for Organizers™
https://www.coachapproachfororganizers.com/organizer_coach_certification.html

Find a Personal Coach

International Coach Federation
https://coachfederation.org/credentialed-coach-finder

Find a Personal Photo Organizer

Association of Personal Photo Organizers
https://www.appo.org/default.aspx

Find a Professional Organizer

The Institute for Challenging Disorganization®
https://www.challengingdisorganization.org

National Association of Productivity and Organizing Professionals℠
https://www.napo.net

Find a Senior Move Manager®

National Association of Senior Move Managers
https://www.nasmm.org/

References

Chapter 1

Cherry, Kendra. 2018. "Fluid Intelligence vs. Crystalized Intelligence." *Very Well Mind*. December 13. https://www.verywellmind.com/fluid-intelligence-vs-crystallized-intelligence-2795004

Chapter 2

Miller, William R. and Stephen Rollnick. 2002. *Motivational Interviewing.* 2nd ed. NY: Guilford.

Prochaska, James O., John Norcross, and Carlo DiClemente. 2006. *Changing for Good.* NY: Harper Collins.

Brown, Brené. 2012. *Daring Greatly: How the Courage to Be Vulnerable Transforms the Way We Live, Love, Parent, and Lead.* NY: Penguin.

Chapter 4

Dahl, Melissa. 2017. "Yes, Shopping Can Be Addictive." *Elle*. January. https://www.elle.com/fashion/shopping/a41845/shopping-dopamine/

Chapter 5

Hendrix, Harville and Helen LaKelly Hunt. 2019. *Getting the Love You Want*, 3rd ed. NY: St. Martin's Griffin. Also view, https://harvilleandhelen.com/initiatives/what-is-imago/

Chapter 6

Bridges, William. 2009. *Managing Transitions: Making the Most of Change*, 3rd ed. Philadelphia, PA: DeCapo Press.

Swift, Art. 2017. "Most U.S. Employed Adults Plan to Work Past Retirement Age." *Gallup*. May 8. https://news.gallup.com/poll/210044/employed-adults-plan-work-past-retirement-age.aspx

Chapter 7

Kolberg, Judith. 2007. *Conquering Chronic Disorganization*, 2nd ed. Decatur, GA: Squall Press.

Kondo, Marie. 2014. *The Life-Changing Magic of Tidying Up*. Berkeley, CA: 10 Speed Press.

Chapter 9

Miller, William R. and Stephen Rollnick. 2002. *Motivational Interviewing*, 2nd ed. NY: Guilford.

Denning, Patt. 2000. *Practicing Harm Reduction Psychotherapy: An Alternative Approach to Addictions*. NY: Guilford Press.

Tompkins, Michael A. and Tamara L Hartl. 2009. *Digging Out: Helping Your Loved One Manage Clutter, Hoarding, and Compulsive Acquiring*. Oakland, CA: New Harbinger.

Chapter 11

Arias, Elizabeth. 2010. "United States Life Tables, 2006." *U.S. Department of Health and Human Services National Vital Statistics Report*. 58, no. 21. (June). https://www.cdc.gov/nchs/data/nvsr/nvsr58/nvsr58_21.pdf

Jarvis, Peter, John Holdford, and Colin Griffin. 2003. *The Theory and Practice of Learning*. 2nd Ed. London: Kogan Page.

Merriam, Sharan B. 2005. "How Adult Life Transitions Foster Learning and Development." *New Directions for Adult and Continuing Education*. 108, 3-13, https://doi.org/10.1002/ace.193

Merriam, Sharan B., Rosemary S. Caffarella, and Lisa M. Baumgartner. 2007. *Learning in Adulthood*. 3rd ed. Hoboken, NJ: John Wiley & Sons.

Chapter 13

Rodden, Janice. 2018. "ADHD May Reduce Life Expectancy By As Much As 13 Years." *ADDitude*. November 18. https://www.additudemag.com/adhd-life-expectancy-russell-barkley/

Holland, Kimberly and Elsbeth Riley. 2017. "ADHD Numbers: Facts, Statistics, and You." October 11. https://www.addrc.org/adhd-numbers-facts-statistics-and-you/

Cowan, Douglas. 2012. "Neurology of ADHD." *ADHD Information Library*. January 22. https://newideas.net/adhd/neurology

Brown, Thomas E. 2005. *Attention Deficit Disorder*. New Haven, CT: Yale UP.

Solden, Sari. 2002. *Journeys Through ADDulthood*. NY: Walker.

Acknowledgments

I am most grateful for my professional organizing colleagues. The friendships built through Coach Approach for Organizers™, the National Association of Productivity and Organizing Professionals℠, and especially the Institute for Challenging Disorganization® have been life-changing. Nettie Owens played a particularly important role during and after an ICD conference, coaching me to believe in my value and this project. My accountability partners, Phyllis Flood Knerr and Terina Bainter, provided invaluable encouragement. There are many more organizing and coaching friends—both old and new—who hold a very special place in my heart. You know who you are.

I appreciate those who have helped me with technical expertise, including downsizing and senior move expert Mary Kay Buysse; personal photo organizer Marci Brennan; ninety-nine-year-old witness to history Glenn Oertley; and car expert Chuck Oertley. The talented Hanne Brøter worked diligently and patiently to create a beautifully designed cover. Last, but not least, I thank my amazing editor, Deborah Kevin, without whom I would still be puttering with these pages. She has been a gift from the Universe.

Finally, I want to thank my family for their encouragement and patience as I went through the intense process of birthing another book, and also my bestie, Shannon. Your support means everything to me.

About the Author

Kate Varness, CPO-CD®, COC®, has been helping clients organize their homes and reach their goals for over fifteen years with her company, Green Light Organizing, and Coaching. Kate has been featured on TheKitchn.com, local television, and in Family Fun, Parents, and Family Circle. A frequent speaker, both locally and nationally, Kate also blogs, has contributed to other organizing books and edited a professional organizer training book. This is her first solo publication. She is the mother of three teens and two sweet dogs.

Made in the USA
San Bernardino, CA
21 March 2019